OXFORD BOY

With Mum and Dad in the
University Parks.

Other books by Will Wyatt:

The Man Who Was B. Traven (Cape, 1980)

The Fun Factory – A Life in the BBC (Aurum Press, 2003)

Contributor to

Masters of the Wired World (Financial Times, 1999)

B. Traven – der (un)bekannte Schriftsteller (Igel Verlag, 2017

OXFORD BOY

A POST-WAR
TOWNIE CHILDHOOD

WILL WYATT

Signal

Signal Books
Oxford

First published in 2018 by
Signal Books Limited
36 Minster Road
Oxford OX4 1LY
www.signalbooks.co.uk

A catalogue record for this book is available from the British Library

ISBN 978-1-909930-64-3 Paper

Cover Design: Baseline Arts, Oxford
Typesetting: Tora Kelly
Cover Image: courtesy Will Wyatt
Printed in India by Imprint Press

For Honey

CONTENTS

INTRODUCTION

"There is always one moment in childhood when the door opens and lets the future in." Graham Greene, *The Power and the Glory*

I have always thought each of us should remember, record and relate what we can of our lives. I have often kept diaries. When my father was widowed I gave him a tape recorder and a list of questions and urged him to respond to them of a winter evening. He did. I had the material transcribed and edited it into a volume for his ninetieth birthday. The big human story, the encyclopaedia of our world, is comprised of our individual stories, everyone unique. The tales will overlap, duplicate and contradict each other. They are not all of equal novelty, significance or fascination, but each places another inimitable pebble on the cairn. I hereby add one more modest volume to the vast library of childhoods.

People often say they are proud of their parents or of their ancestry, that they come from a long line of miners or sailors or dukes, that the family have lived in Appleby or Hackney or Aberdeenshire for generations, that the estate has been in the family for centuries. All interesting but why should they be proud of something they have had no influence on, no say in and done nothing to bring about? The *Shorter Oxford English Dictionary* has pride as "a feeling of elation or high satisfaction derived from some action or possession". Quite so. Our ancestry, our parents, derive from no action of ours and they are in no way a possession. So I don't feel I have the right to be proud of my parents but I do know that I was lucky to have them. I hope

1

they were proud of me in that I most certainly derived from their actions and they had every reason to be proud of themselves. In the same way, I can't claim I am proud to have been born and brought up in Oxford, much as I love the city. I just turned up there and then came to understand how fortunate I was.

I had the idea of writing this book after standing next in the gents to Bryan Magee, philosopher, politician, writer and broadcaster.

"What are you writing at the moment?" I asked.

"I am writing about my childhood," said Bryan, adding, "Up to the age of nine."

"Golly, how vain," I replied discourteously, meaning only that there must be an awful lot of volumes to come. He was understandably put out. That book was *Clouds of Glory*, a vivid account of his boyhood in Hoxton, then a crime-ridden slum. I can in no way emulate Bryan's achievement in that book but it did plant the seed. I had long intended to write something about the eleven plus shenanigans and doorway it provided. Bryan's work encouraged me to go beyond.

I have sought to indicate where my memory may not be sound; where I have been able to check I have done so. Nevertheless, I know that I will have made errors – only small ones, I hope - for which I apologise in advance. Memory is fallible, tells us fibs and repeats its own legends. If I have been unfair to anyone, well, that's how they seemed to this boy at the time. Some names have been changed; most haven't.

My memory of the family was jogged and gaps coloured in by my brother, David, and my cousin, Anne Bennett, with a jot or two added by Mick Wyatt, Ron Wyatt and Charlotte Hooper. School memories were prompted and augmented by John Cooke, Robert Herbertson, Tim Hunt, Alan Pemberton, Laurence Simmons and Richard Warnock. My thanks to all.

Eddie Mirzoeff was generous enough to read the whole manuscript and provide blunt criticism as well as encouragement and valuable suggestions; Iain Johnstone did the same for one or two early chapters. They improved what I had written and saved some embarrassments.

For the chapters about Magdalen College School I leaned upon D.L.L. Clarke's updating of the school history and purloined material about Bob Stanier from his wife Maida's *Portrait of a Schoolmaster*.

One other person read every word and discussed them with me, my wife Jane. She knows that my thanks to her include this but run far wider and deeper.

May Day at Phil and Jim primary school. WW in profile third left of standing boys. I may have been partner to Valerie Gardiner.

1
THE POINT OF A PENCIL

normally had no reason to return to school after hours. We had no homework, no clubs, no after school games. In the summer, I would play in the garden with my brother, walk to Port Meadow to fish or to the University Parks to watch cricket. In winter, I would stay warm inside to play with model soldiers and Dinky toys or watch the newly arrived television. So my short journey this late afternoon in March 1953 was unusual. From our front door I crossed Kingston Road to Sibley's electrical shop on the corner opposite and then walked a hundred yards or so along Leckford Road, passing the spot where I once tried shoe skating on the ice-covered pavement and had fallen, chipping my new front tooth. I turned into Leckford Place to the school gate carrying only my pencil case and a rubber. It was a walk that would determine much of the rest of my life.

Earlier in the day I had sat the eleven plus examination at SS Philip and James Church of England Primary School, "Phil and Jim". Our headmaster, Mr Gray, had told me to return later with the same writing implements I had used in the exam. Another boy was there, as well. Otherwise the school was empty and quiet. Now, Mr Gray led us to his study and produced the maths and intelligence papers we had completed that morning. He pointed out some questions we had answered wrongly and all but held our pencils as we corrected them. Were there lots of mistakes to correct? I cannot recall. I am sure there were enough to make the exercise meaningful. Was I aware that something that should not happen was happening? I am not sure. There must have been a conspiratorial air to the occasion but I was crossing none of the lines that marked good from bad for me then. This was my headmaster and I was doing his bidding. My parents knew I had been summoned back after hours and seemed to think it was a good idea. They had even been out for a drink with Mr Gray and his attractive wife.

But there were only two of us boys present. Where were my other friends? Did I know if they were summoned back as well? If I thought about it at all I must have assumed not. Did I fret about being picked out in this way? I don't think so. I was a goody-goody boy and keen to please. I went along with it all. We were not there long. Mr Gray seemed satisfied with the changes we had made and the other boy and I went our separate ways home.

Some weeks earlier I had been told to write a composition on the subject of "Oxford", the city in which we lived. I handed in my work and Mr. Gray took me through it suggesting some improvements. In particular, he said to end the essay with a flourish, "from the motor car factory at Cowley to the cobble stones of Merton Street." I rewrote the essay with just that ending. These were certainly not my own words. Everybody in Oxford knew about Morris Motors factory but I had never been to Merton Street and this was the first I had heard of cobble stones there. My new version was deemed satisfactory and Mr Gray had said, "Memorise it." I did and thought no more about it. Lo and behold, when I came to sit the eleven plus the subject we were asked to write a composition on was "My Home Town". I delivered. The results would be known in a couple of months.

Phil and Jim was a small, very urban school with a brick and concrete air raid shelter under the big chestnut tree by the street wall. It was mixed to the age of seven then one form per year of boys only from eleven to the school leaving age of fifteen. A.G.B. Gray, proudly ex RAF, was head of this boys' school. He was cheery, buoyant presence, a portly man with crinkly black hair. Yet we feared him. He loped around the school in the fat man's way with arms dangling straight, palms facing to the rear. Unless, that is, he was patrolling with his cane. Armed in this way, he came across an older boy called Trego whistling in the corridor and whacked him about the head and shoulders for this, or so the story ran round the school.

I had begun at the mixed infants next door when I was three and a half under the kindly care of Miss Brucker. I remember an immensely tall woman, silver hair in a bun, riding a sit up and beg bicycle to and from school. On my first day I had to be fetched home crying, the emotion of which rather than any detail I remember. We learned reading and writing before a daily rest on camp beds. Miss Marston's class was next. She was severe of aspect but not of manner. We sat at individual desks arranged in rows before her. She taught us sums, impressing the need for neatness. I have the image of her carrying the teachers' mid-morning drink, a large cup of steaming hot milk with Camp Coffee, a brown mostly chicory liquid added from a bottle. The smell lingers.

The headmistress of the infants was the distant and strict Miss Hodge. She had an adopted son, Joscelyn, a name we had some difficulty with as we knew of a girl called Joscelyn and any idiot knew you simply could not call a boy by a girl's name. We only caught glimpses of Joscelyn for he went to a different school, one you paid for someone said. I think Miss Hodge was probably a very good teacher. She certainly ran a tight ship. An older boy called Schofield, who came from Jericho way, borrowed another's boy's bike for a ride or rather "stole it" according to the charge sheet. Miss Hodge believed punishment should be witnessed as well as undergone. She put a chair in front of the class and tied Schofield to it with some rope, gagging him with a yellow black board duster fastened behind his head. There he remained for the afternoon. I felt sorry for him. He was often in trouble. It wasn't so much that he did not have a bike - few boys had them - but I sensed there were quite a few things Schofield did not have.

THE POINT OF A PENCIL

I fell foul of Miss Hodge on a couple of occasions. She caught another boy and me dropping our pencils on the floor so we could get under the big desk to see the girls' knickers. For this we had to write out lines, "I must not behave so badly in class". I didn't like this and in a moment of bravado exclaimed, "Damn these lines" in a voice loud enough for Miss Hodge to hear. The word "damn" prompted her to grab my ear and lead me by it out of the class to the cloakroom nearby. There she pushed my head down into a basin, ran the tap and washed out my mouth with soap and water. As a strategy for cleaning up my language this literalist approach failed. She had to do the same thing all over again a month or so later and I have been pretty foul mouthed for most of my life. She didn't threaten me as she did my brother when he refused to eat his slimy mashed potato at school dinner. "Jesus puts a black cross on the forehead of bad boys," she said, standing over him till he finished it, gagging on every mouthful.

A highlight of the year was May Day. This was not for any political reason but as a folksy festive occasion when the six and seven year olds would dance round the maypole in front of the parents. The first year I was to be part of this was a disaster. We had rehearsed skip dancing this way and that, passing the red, white and blue ribbons over and under until they made a satisfying plait at the top of the pole. On the morning of the great day I rushed into the boys' lavatory for a pee but in an excited hurry instead of turning the corner inside to the pee gutter, I simply peed up against the wall at the back. Horror of horrors, I was spotted by some tell-tale girls who dashed to teacher to describe the disgusting sight they had witnessed. Sight of what? The back of a six-year-old and his damp stream. It was more than enough. I was to be shamed, dropped from the maypole dance and sent inside to sit it out on my own.

I did make the dance the following year and there is a photograph to prove it. The maypole was raised in the centre of the small concrete playground between the infants' school and the church hall where school dinners were served. Shortly before twelve o'clock, the hot food arrived in great steel containers delivered by van from some central kitchen. Save for a very few occasions I happily avoided the contents of these threatening vessels as I could walk home for dinner.

When we were seven the girls disappeared and we went into the big boys' school next door, a fence separating the playgrounds. Here the teachers were all male. Rumours of terrible rituals for newcomers were not borne out and we began in the cosy class of Mr Cox. "Old Cocker" seemed awfully old. He bicycled so slowly up Leckford Road that he seemed bound to wobble off. He spoke with a soft Berkshire accent and told us stories of the ancient Britons on the Ridgeway, the legend of Wayland's Smithy and the Blowing Stone with which King Alfred was said to have summoned his troops, all features of his native heath out near Wantage. For nature study we were issued folders, alternating pages of thick grey paper and tissue, in which I pressed wild flowers: bird's-foot trefoil, speedwell, tufted vetch, shepherd's purse, buttercups, scarlet pimpernels, yarrow, cornflowers and scabious.

I loved the history tales and the flowers but Cocker's special hobby did not hook me in the same way. He made miniature steam engines, not railway -engines but little jewel-like stationary engines of brass and copper. When fed with water and fuelled by tiny lumps of coal or methylated spirits, they puffed smoke from the chimney and powered a polished shaft. I could admire but making such things was beyond me. I came top of Cocker's small class. His comment was, "Has done a good year's work but his work is not always neat enough". And so it was always to be.

Mr Phillips, a specialist in handicrafts, took the next year up. He was a slim pale-skinned man and I was fascinated by the fair hairs on the back of his hand as he sought to help me in the mysteries of raffia work. Under his tutelage, I was able to make a basket or two but that was about it. Mr Phillips caned us on our upturned hands. We would involuntarily draw the palm back and forth as if trying to balance an invisible pencil in anticipation of the pain. He had mastered an impressive whippy action and rarely missed the palm.

In the mornings we lined up by class in the playground and on the sound of a whistle marched into the school, top class first. Sports were limited given the size of the school estate. There was PE sometimes in the playground when it was dry. We played cricket there with a tennis ball and stumps drawn on the wall. Later, we were taken as a treat to play football on the bumpy grass of Port Meadow, a huge area of open pasture booby-trapped with cowpats and horse poo. In the holidays we even managed cricket there with a slight mound serving as our pavilion and grandstand.

There was much excitement when Mr Gray arranged a football match against Wolvercote School. For this Phil and Jim provided us with proper jerseys, dark blue and light blue quarters. These colours carried a charge. The university did not touch my world directly but you couldn't be a boy in Oxford without supporting the dark blues against the Cambridge light blues, in the boat race above all, but also the cricket and rugby matches. And then there was Pegasus, an amateur football team comprising former Oxford and Cambridge blues, which was based in Oxford and cutting a dash in the then high-profile amateur football world. Dad used to take me with him to watch them play on the Iffley Road pitch and I glowed when he knew a lot of people in the crowd. "Who was that, Dad?" "He works for Hinkins and Frewin." Or "He's one of the Coppocks."

Or "That's old so and so. He used to spit in our blacking," which I learned was someone you knew but not that well. The Pegs won the FA Amateur Cup in 1951 and 1953 in front of 100,000 capacity crowds at Wembley, Dad and I among them. (The programme recorded the schools and Oxbridge colleges of the Pegasus players.) They played in flapping white shirts but were the dark and light blues in every other way. Wolvercote School had its own pitch with goal posts so this was our big time. There were even people shouting on the touchline. We lost but did not let our proud colours down.

An ambitious cricket fixture at the Dragon School, Oxford's most famous prep school, was rather different. We only ever played cricket in the playground or midst the cow pats of Port Meadow so this was to be the first time we had experienced wooden stumps and umpires. Although not much more than a quarter of a mile away the Dragon was terra incognita. None of us knew anyone who went there. This was an upwardly mobile move by Mr Gray. I am not sure which of the Dragon's many teams we played, certainly not the first.

We arrived at their extensive grounds excited and apprehensive. It was all like the real thing, hard ball, pads, the lot. They batted first. The one thing I was particularly good at was catching so it was mortifying when one of their early batsmen put up a dolly to me at mid-off and I dropped it. No matter, they were all out for "only" 116 which, everyone agreed, was jolly good going on our part. There was a tea with sandwiches, then we went in and were all out for just sixteen. We felt and were humiliated, not least because they were all so insufferably, bloody nice about it. Shouts of "hard luck" and "just when you looked set" at each display of incompetence. Even at ten I knew we were being patronised. The match was a kind of social work for the Dragon. A dim thought struggled to tell me that there might be more of this in life and I would have to deal with it.

Phil and Jim was in Leckford Road on the border of poshest North Oxford and the more modest houses of what estate agents now dub Walton Manor. Some, probably less well-off, dons did send their sons to the school but most boys were very much townies. Of my chums' fathers, one was the verger at St Giles' Church, one worked at the Clarendon Printers, another worked at Morris's. Mind you, Jeremy Taylor's dad did go to work in a suit. Few displayed any signs of money but we knew that the poorer boys wore black plimsolls rather than shoes or summer sandals and came from Jericho, streets of urban cottages off Walton Street. Their school should have been Barney, St Barnabas, where we knew the boys were much rougher and tougher than us.

Jeremy Taylor was my best friend. His garden backed onto the Oxford Canal and we could fish there. One hot summer afternoon after school, he and I had an almighty, sweaty, fight on the corner of Leckford and Kingston Roads, both crying from effort and frustration. Neil Butler was a spindly boy with specs, prone to tears and a sulk when given out at cricket. He owned the bat and ball but we would not let him take them home. He would hang about sobbing till he ingratiated himself back into the game by doing a bit of desultory fielding. We let him join in again as if nothing had happened. Terry Collier, born on exactly the same day as me, was tall and athletic and went to a proper swimming club. Michael Hagerty was an eager bouncy fellow. "Hey, that's genuine spam," he exclaimed when I showed him what was in my sandwiches on a coach outing to the anti-climax that was "California in England." I remember him standing back from a painting he had done in class and asking in his best grown up way, "Shall I give it another coat?" Tony Faulkner's dark hair flopped into his right eye and my mum said he would need glasses soon. And he did.

OXFORD BOY

Tony Belcher and I were best playground chums, galloping synchronously, arms linked behind our backs on noble adventures. Alan Whitaker was a tall, kindly friend who played brass musical instruments and made model aircraft. Pipsy Parsons was an impish boy with a small face and fair hair like a pile of pancakes on his head. When in February 1952 Mr Gray opened the door of our class interrupting the lesson to tell us solemnly that the King had died that morning, Pipsy looked round the room and grinned. It was the excited grin of one aware that something momentous was taking place but the head was furious. He gave Pipsy a serious caning. I don't remember much bullying. There was a big boy called Parker who lived in a large house directly opposite the school. He was sent home by the headmaster several times for thumping someone or losing his temper. But he's the one I remember crying and even on one occasion running out of the school and back home across the road.

There was poor Cleghorn, an awkward boy with few friends. He invited a number of us to his birthday party which was to be held on a Saturday in a Chinese restaurant in the middle of the city. This was an exotic invitation. Birthday parties, when they were held at all, were just jelly and cakes and running riot in the birthday boy's house, possibly with a game or two, musical chairs or the Hokey Cokey. I had never been to a restaurant. That it was to be Chinese was a worry but Cleghorn informed us that it would be all right. My mum bought a present for me to take, a wooden pencil box, the top half of which swivelled to reveal a bottom compartment. At four o'clock on the Saturday all the invited boys assembled with a parent outside the restaurant. By half past four it was evident that Cleghorn was not going to show. The restaurant knew nothing. There was no party. He had made it up. We went home.

At school on Monday we reassembled and held a council of war. Yes, we were going to "get" Cleghorn. We told him to hide somewhere at playtime and warned him that if we found him the "getting" would take place. The playground was small and other than going round a corner of the building, easily checked, the only possible hiding spots were behind a couple of scrubby bushes. Sure enough we straightway saw that he was stooping behind one of these. Yet, without discussing it, none of us let on that we knew where he was. We caught each other's eye and an act of clemency was passed without a word spoken. I used the pencil box myself.

We had playground games other than cricket and "footer" as we called it. We collected fag cards, sets of picture cards of sportsmen, figures from history, regimental badges and uniforms, film stars, aeroplanes, kings and queens, cars, railway engines et al, which came in cigarette packets. With these we played "knock downs" and "on tops", flicking the card to hit a target card propped against a wall or trying to cover cards on the ground. Success meant you picked up all the relevant cards in play. Such games did nothing for the condition of the cards which for us were for playing with not sticking in albums.

In September conkers ruled. With a kitchen skewer you made a hole through the glossy brown fruit of the horse chestnut, threaded it with a foot-long piece of string and tied a knot below. You were then ready to challenge or be challenged by another conker owner. After a cry of "Iddy iddy onker my first conker, iddy iddy oh my first go" each took alternate turns at striking the top of the other's conker with a downward swing of one's own until one or other broke up. If both conkers were virgin combatants the winner would now be a "twoer", if the loser had been already a "fourer", say, the winner became a "fiver". Some weapons were gnarled from oven baking or soaking in vinegar, both frowned upon but common.

In winter, we would take a run to slide on a long patch of ice in the playground, grandstanding to perform "little man" or "one foot". We were cowboys, knights and other heroes galloping in pairs and in step, arms linked behind our backs, wind in our hair as we raced and rescued. Occasionally there would be massive game of bums and barrels. Each member of one team would bend head down making a back, one behind the other, head to bum, in a line from a wall. A member of the other team ran to jump onto the backs wiggling himself forward towards the wall. Then the next player and the next till the line of backs collapsed under the weight. There were laughs, tears and cries of pain. Injuries were rarely more than bloody knees from the gritty playground. We all wore grey flannel short trousers and my knees were permanently encrusted with scabs from grazes. These one absent-mindedly ran a finger over relishing the smooth pitted surface before slowly picking, lifting it off in one piece if possible. Even more satisfying than picking one's nose.

We were taken by coach for swimming lessons at Temple Cowley Baths, nearly half an hour away. The swimming was fun but there lurked a terror of what one might catch at the pool. The word "verruca" cast an ominous shadow. I never saw one, never had one and I never heard that any of the others boys did, but "verruca" and "swimming pool" went together like tooth ache and sweets. I did get my certificate for swimming across the pool, ten yards, and another for swimming a length, 25 yards. The worst thing that happened on a swimming trip was when I fell out of the emergency door of the coach as it swung left from Woodstock Road into Bevington Road. I crashed onto the curb. Fortunately, there was no vehicle following and I rose and walked clutching my left side towards the now stationary coach and a worried looking teacher. There must have been some sort of examination back at the school but the only treatment I had was to be taken home for the rest of the day.

The teacher on the coach was Mr Rowley, now my class teacher. I liked Mr Rowley and under him I came top again. He had a boyish face, fair floppy hair and a cheery laugh. The curriculum was religious knowledge, English - reading aloud, dictation, composition, poetry and speech - history (my favourite subject), geography, "elementary science including nature study, hygiene", crafts, PT, (physical training), music and arithmetic including mental arithmetic. Mr Rowley drove a Rover, a cut above any other car we knew the owner of. He was proud of it and sought successfully to impress us with the average speed he had achieved on a drive from York to Oxford, a figure he made us work out for ourselves. It was about twenty miles per hour.

In the late spring of 1953 my parents received a letter from the Oxford Education Committee; "On the results of the Annual Schools Examination it has been decided that your child Alan [as I was christened] Wyatt is suitable for admission to a secondary (grammar) school." It asked them to choose from the list of three schools and promised "free tuition and books irrespective of the parents' financial circumstances".

In Oxford the eleven plus was not simply pass or fail. Everyone knew there was a hierarchy of passes. At the top was Magdalen College School, a direct grant school, which meant that half the places were fee paying and the other half awarded free on the results of the eleven plus, half of these thirty or so free places going to boys from the city, half to boys from the county. This was my parents' first choice. The other two, the excellent City of Oxford High School and perfectly good Southfield School in that order, were both entirely free grammar schools. A second letter confirmed that I had been accepted for Magdalen. Mum and Dad were thrilled. This is what it had all been about, getting two boys from Phil and Jim into the top school. Mr Gray had no children of his own. Was he simply making sure that a couple of bright boys got the best possible leg up in life? Or was it swagger? Look what a great school that Mr Gray runs! Two boys to Magdalen this year! Certainly, the latter, probably both.

The summer term was a happy one. Mr and Mrs Gray joined some of our neighbours to watch the Coronation on the television set we had owned for a year or more. Mum served ham sandwiches and beer. A British expedition climbed Everest and *The Eagle* comic illustrated the route they had taken. We children were told often that The New Elizabethan age had arrived. England won back the Ashes, the dashing Denis Compton hitting the winning runs. All was well with the world.

My class teacher that last year at Phil and Jim was the quiet and dignified Mr Flello, whose gentle authority I remember fondly. I have still the form prize he gave me, two volumes of *The Concise History of Britain*, which came in useful for notes and essays at my new school. His unusual name has allowed me to look him up and discover that he had spent three years as a prisoner of the Japanese. Had we boys known this at the time it would have impressed us greatly. It impresses me now. There were no leaving ceremonies at primary schools in those days. Celebrations of any success were muted, no leaping about, air punching or whooping. No special assembly, no parents' event, no concert. Most of my friends were going to the High School or Southfield, one or two to a new technical school, Cheney, and one or two just stayed on at the secondary modern rump, tiny as it was, of Phil and Jim.

Did I feel guilty about what had helped me along? After all I was above the age of criminal responsibility, old enough to be arrested and charged with a crime. But, no, I didn't. Somehow it had just happened and I took it for granted. At eleven what is, just is. Did I feel guilty later and do I feel guilty now? I would much rather I had sailed to Magdalen without the cheating but guilty, no. Would I have gone anyway? Impossible to know, but probably not if I had to bet. Whose place did I then take? Another impossible question. In my defence, or perhaps in Mr Gray's defence, I did not waste the place. I flourished at the new school. Not a strong defence I accept: pleading guilty to stealing with mitigating circumstances, namely that you spent the money wisely.

Was Mr Gray lucky to get away with it? Were lots of heads at it? Not long ago I saw a story in the press, "A head teacher was jailed today for changing pupils' exam answers because he thought they had more ability than they showed, Judge Keith Simpson said 'The damage that can be done by this sort of activity should never be underestimated. If others behaved in that way the whole system would be utterly destroyed - and that cannot happen.'" Such tales crop up from time to time.

A few years ago I told the story of my eleven plus to an Oxford professor who was neither shocked nor surprised. She straightway replied, "Yes, I cheated in my eleven plus, too. When I sat the maths paper, I saw questions which had figures and dots in between. I'd never seen these before. So, I put up my hand and said I was feeling terribly ill. I was taken out and my mother came to fetch me. She rang up my uncle who was a doctor and he provided me with a medical certificate which confirmed I was ill. I was, thus, allowed to re-sit the examination several weeks later after an intensive course of private coaching in decimals." There must have been many more.

From the outcome of that eleven plus exam I can trace a direct line determining the thing most important to me, my family. All our lives are full of might-have-beens and what ifs, moments when a small decision or chance led to a string of consequences. Some are trivial: "if I'd not had a coffee in that café I would not have heard someone talking about that author who is now my favourite." Some are life changing: "I was last to arrive and took the only seat remaining on the coach next to the man who gave me my first job." The film *Sliding Doors* played out two different lives of a woman decided by her just catching or just missing a tube train. Robert Frost's poem "The Road Not Taken" considers how a moment of capricious choice can dictate a life:

> *Two roads diverged in a wood, and I—*
> *I took the one less traveled by,*
> *And that has made all the difference.*

Mr Gray's eleven plus scam was not a stroke of chance, though like everyone else I have experienced a share. It was not a shall I, shan't I, might as well go this way decision. It was a plot, albeit one I entered into unconsciously. And when I consider my daughters or my granddaughter they are the direct result. Without the cheating they would not exist and my life would be immeasurably poorer.

For without Mr Gray's scheme I'm sure I would have passed the eleven plus but at a lower level. I would probably have gone to the City of Oxford High School, where I would likely have prospered. But would any teacher there have given me such an edge as to exceed my abilities as Peter Arnold-Craft did at Magdalen College School? Unlikely, but possible. In which case, I would have found my way to university, Oxford even and who knows, on to journalism and the BBC. But most certainly Dr Peter Brooks would not have taught me and it was he who suggested I apply to

Emmanuel College, Cambridge. I knew nothing of the college and without Dr Brooks would never have thought of it. Had I not gone to Emma, I would not have been placed in the next room to fellow scholar Richard Archer. No Richard, then I would not have shared War on Want lunches with his school friend Joe Tatton-Brown. No Joe, and I would never have met his Hertfordshire neighbour, Cathy Wells. No Cathy Wells, no best friend of hers, Jane Bagenal. No Jane, no daughters, Hannah and Rozzy, and no fifty-year marriage; no Rozzy, no granddaughter, Honey.

How could I feel that this should not have happened? The whole of a life balanced on the point of a sharpened pencil.

A swimming picnic at Sandy Bay, on Port Meadow. WW with Mum c. 1945.

2.
A BIT OF EXTRA FLAVOUR

Might there have been no eleven plus for me? Did I nearly die in a road accident? Was I already at the age of four the beneficiary of a stroke of good fortune, lucky to be alive? I thought so. I used to tell my friends how I rolled under a number three bus in Kingston Road and lay on the tarmac as the bus passed over me. I described to them and to myself the sensations of the road, the noise, the large wheels and the dark underneath of the bus, all clear in my mind. I told of how I was picked up unscathed, a miraculous escape. I had heard my mother telling people how "our Alan fell under a bus" and believed exactly what she said. From this I developed for myself a vivid memory of the drama. I did ride my tricycle along the pavement outside our house and must have once fallen off and over the edge of the curb when a bus was near. "Under a bus" was a near enough account, I suppose. It was only when I grew up that I realised that what I had remembered so clearly could never have happened.

If I was not snatched from the jaws of death on Kingston Road I had been snatched a little too carelessly when, as a breech baby, I first thrust my bottom at the world. My neck was injured so that my head would lean heavily to one side when I became tired. I never heard my parents suggest that the North Oxford Nursing Home was at fault, but the place left much to be desired. Dad had dug deep to pay for it in the belief that his wife, Hettie, would be well looked after in such an establishment. This was not to be. Mum was left for long periods and was frightened she would be on her own when the baby arrived. There was a bell but it was not often answered by the nurse. Visiting times as in other hospitals in those We-Know-Best days were grudging and policed, two till four thirty and then at six. The weather was cold, Dad came on foot or by bus and at half past four he refused to leave. "I thought,

I'm not going back. By the time I gets home it will be time to come again." The nurse would get upset, "but I didn't go. I thought bugger, I'm not having that."

The doctors waited till I was three to operate on my neck. Again, visiting hours were mean and left a searing memory. The Wingfield Orthopaedic Hospital was in Windmill Road, Cowley, a long way from our home. Mum and Dad were to come on the Sunday afternoon, driven by my Uncle Arthur in his car. In the children's ward I waited eagerly for visiting time but this came and ended with no one to see me. I was downcast as all the other parents left. A while later, through the glass of the door I saw the faces I hoped for: Mum's long face with its strong, almost Roman nose and the egg-shaped head of Dad, already quite bald but whose pencil moustache was then still dark as his hair had been. They could only wave and silently mouth to me. The hospital staff would not allow them in. They must have visited another time but it is that disappointment that scarred the memory. Even now I am easily affected by stories of children let down by adults, whether true or fictional. I was loved. Mum and Dad did eventually turn up. I do not remember them ever letting me down again and I learned that this time was not their fault, the car had broken down. There are thousands of children whose disappointments are more serious, are repeated and which are not resolved. If my small incident left such a mark, what of theirs?

The one pleasant memory of that hospital stay was being given a warm and blissfully comforting drink from the spout of a special cup. The gratifying sensation remained with me but I never encountered the nectar again. Never, that is, until I was around seventeen and thirsty in the tea interval of a cricket match. In the absence of my favoured orange squash I decided to try what everyone else was drinking, a cup of tea with a little milk and sugar. At the first mouthful it came back to me. I knew where I had tasted it before, it was the nectar from the special cup, sweet tea. The odd thing was I had never liked tea or thought I didn't. For whatever reason, I had unconsciously taken care not to drink it.

The operation left me cased in plaster from neck to waist. For some weeks I couldn't move my neck to see what I was eating so had to be fed: "Some egg next. A bit of bread. Some milk." I can't have been easy for my mother to handle in the plaster jacket. Eventually, the doctors decided it could come off and with a lot of cutting and creaking, I was free. My neck was fine thereafter.

The house I was brought home to was 15 Kingston Road, which we rented from G. T. Jones, the long standing Oxford wine merchants who had a shop on the ground floor. Mum was manageress of the shop, which opened from ten thirty to two and from six to seven in the evening. I think that Mum, who was nearly 35 when she had me, found motherhood a bit of strain. She had a little help. Emily from Jericho came twice a week to do some housework and one of Mum's customers, Mrs Cornhill - "Corny"- a nice elderly lady, occasionally lent a hand. Mr Jones sent someone up in the mornings to open the shop and Dad served there in the evening when he got home from work bricklaying. Soon Mum was able to take over again, my pram parked in front of the shop window where she could keep an eye on me.

When they had married in 1935 Mum and Dad had saved up for a mortgage on a three-bedroom semi-detached house on the Eynsham Road, newly built by Mum's brother Walter. It was the last but one house on the left leaving Oxford. She had cycled the three miles to and from work from there but would get soaked through at times and developed rheumatism. So when after two years part of 15 Kingston Road became free they rented that for a modest sum and let out the house they owned.

Kingston Road is an extension of Walton Street running north from the centre of the city more or less parallel to the much grander Woodstock Road. It is part of the North Oxford suburb developed between 1860 and the end of the century on the St John's College estate. There are many imposing Gothic and Italianate villas but Kingston and the roads near it comprise mostly terraces of two-, three- and four-story houses. It was not a busy road but was served by the number three bus which ran from Iffley though the city centre, along Walton Street and for a couple of stops past us to turn round at St Margaret's Road. Number 15 was four storeys including the basement. Our living room was in the front basement under the shop. We ate at a table in here, before a coal fire in winter. Either side of the fireplace were two armchairs. Dad sat to the right and I have a cosy memory of sitting on his lap as he read a Rupert Bear book to me. He used to call me "my ducker". A rounded 1930s wooden case clock stood on the shelf above the fireplace; the radio presided on a small sideboard, a black and white portrait of Winston Churchill gazed down on us. In my early years the room was lit by gas lights on the wall. They held delicately perforated white mantels like tiny Chinese lanterns which glowed when lit with a spill ignited from the burning coal. Once a week Mum brought the hip bath in before the fire, filled it with water heated in the kitchen and I had my bath. Hot soapy water, shoulders flushed from the fire, the smell of coal, an enveloping towel from a mother's hands; why does childhood have to end?

This was a gloomy room. It had two windows but they looked out at the brick wall of the area and up to lattice like cast iron railings with just glimpses of passers-by and the sky. Over the years,

Mum became fed up with this subterranean view. She felt cooped up, cut off from the goings on in the street. "I've had enough of these four walls," was her repeated complaint. When Dad was late home from work she would vainly peer out at this limited aspect, exuding anxiety. Then I worried too. Had there been an accident? An injury at work? Was something up? No, just a problem at the site or the fog delaying him a little.

Behind this living room was a small space off which was a narrow kitchen. Food was kept in the larder next door where a wooden safe with a perforated zinc front protected milk, fats, meat and so on from flies. From the foot of the stairs a passage towards the front led to the coal hole. The coal man delivered by horse and cart and emptied the thick woven sacks through a manhole with an echoing crash into the store below. It was a dark and unwelcoming place but I would push the door open to gaze at the pile of glistening lumps and take in the smell.

To the rear was another passage leading to the back door and the lavatory. As I sat in there one Christmas Eve looking up through the window I distinctly saw Father Christmas's sleigh. It was moving north to south high across the night sky as he flew to begin his rounds. I reported the sighting and was reminded that it was wise to go to bed in good time so I would not miss his call on our road. To the right of this passage was a cupboard under the stairs known as the "recess" or "the creasess" to Emily, always "Little Emily", who came to help in the house. Here were stored the brooms, the ironing board and hip bath.

Out of the back door was the small bricked area where Mum did her mangling on washday. I liked to watch the two thick wooden rollers squeeze the syrup-like soapy water from the crushed garments. You could run your finger along the sticky surface of the rollers afterwards, being careful of splinters. A few steps led up to the garden. To the right in front of the low wall which separated us from next door was a flower bed where grew marigolds, asters and, Mum's favourite, the scented lilies of the valley. We had two rabbits in a hutch at one time. I used to open the wire cage front not to pet them but to eat the dry bread put there as part of their food. Were they pets? I don't remember them being stroked. Were they eaten? We certainly had rabbit pie now and then, it was a favourite. Surely that was made with wild rabbits, probably shot by Uncle Stan? Perhaps the caged rabbits starved from shortage of food. I still like stale bread.

An old pear tree stood in the centre of a small grassy patch, an important landmark in games of cowboys and Indians, a post to which prisoners could be tied. There was enough muddy grass for it to serve as a pitch for goalmouth scrambles. These comprised last ditch dives and other excuses for falling about dramatically, homage one might think to all that was wrong with English football. At the bottom of the garden a back gate led to the alley beyond and on the left a large rickety shed in which Dad kept things for his work - paints, brushes, a ladder or two, timber. This was the scene of many games out of sight of any grown-ups. My friend Jeremy Taylor and I would make a small fire and drop worms into a heated saucepan to watch them wriggle until they wriggled no more.

When I was five I was standing on the low wall that separated us from number 16 in a cowboy game involving a rope. I think I had been lassoed by a big girl next door and in a brave struggle to free myself and get back to my posse I fell painfully into the flower bed. I went inside to tell Mum that my arm hurt. She put on a coat and led me across the road to catch a bus to the Radcliffe Infirmary half a mile towards the centre of town. On board I sat in pain holding my right arm and heard Mum tell a woman who inquired about me that "I think he has broken his arm." This gave me pause and I asked quite logically, "Will it fall off? Will it fall off?" It was broken and it did not fall off. We alighted at the Clarendon Press and walked through the rear of the hospital buildings to the entrance to what was then called Casualty, where my arm was put in plaster. To this day I have the small scar where my arm must have hit a brick in the fall.

Inside our house, we went upstairs from the living room to reach the hall and the rounded front door which allowed light from three glass panes near the top. There was a door into the shop through which I have no memory of ever going. Behind the shop was what became Mum and Dad's bedroom. Up again to the half landing with a little washroom and a wooden seated lavatory. One day, to great excitement, these became a bathroom with an Ascot water heater. The hip bath was no more. Around the same time the gas lamps also went and in came electricity. Odd that a single bulb casting its bland light from the centre of a room brought such a sense of magic at the time.

My bedroom was at the back on the first floor looking out over the garden. At the front on this floor was the lounge, the largest and brightest room in the house with the generous windows. It looked out to the corner of Leckford Road which ran east from us up past my school and on to Phil and Jim church. The house on the triangular corner plot was the most imposing around. I think we thought the people who lived there a bit snooty. On the near corner of Kingston Road and Longworth Road was a police telephone, a pillar with an iron box at head height which when unlocked by the constable gave him access to that relatively rare apparatus, a telephone. A metal pea shooter was a standard issue weapon for small boys in those days and by raising the sash window in the lounge I could point mine down to the street. To use the phone, the constable needed to turn his back and I could fire a dried pea at him and duck out of sight. If I was lucky I heard it ping off the helmet. Of course, I told stories of how it stung the back of his neck and made him curse and look round, none of which could I have seen if it had.

For the first couple of years that Mum and Dad lived in this house an elderly lady, Miss Turner, occupied these two rooms on the first floor. Mum and Dad had the basement, the room behind the shop and the three rooms on the second floor, which Dad did up to let out. They would go to Miss Florey's house four doors away for a bath each week, as they had only the little wash room. Miss Edith Florey, a round, soft voiced woman with a halo of grey hair, became my godmother, Auntie Florey to us. She never forgot a birthday sending a ten bob note inside a card signed from "Auntie Edith" and sometimes in her Oxford town accent would say "Here, Alan, go arn." And slip me a tip. Looking back she was our closest contact with the university for she ran, as did many neighbours, a registered lodging house for undergraduates.

The top floor lets in our house were never to university people and had not begun well. "The first one, a fellow of about 25, used to play the concertina in the evenings," said Dad, "so he only lasted about two weeks." Then came a middle-aged woman. "She'd been with us about three days and came down to tell Hettie [Mum] that she had arranged for a party with ten or twelve people. When Hettie told me, I went up and laid the law down to her. 'They'll have to come. I've sent out the invitations now,' she said. I said, 'If you wants (sic) that number, you'd better hire the town hall, you won't do it here. I think the best thing that you can do is take a week's notice.'" The woman who came next began changing the furniture around. "That didn't suit Mum," said Dad. "So she only lasted about two weeks." There was then a long pause. My own first memories of the top floor tenants are of two nurses, Miss Winfield and Miss Pitcher, who were with us a while. "Very quiet, no bother, never had anyone in much," said Dad. They kept in touch for many years after.

Next door to us, on the corner of Longworth Road, was Job's Dairy, both a shop and milk distribution business. They began work at four or five in the morning the milkmen unloading milk churns, bottling the milk, filling, loading and clanging the metal crates before their rounds. It was a terrible racket but one we were used to. The alley at the bottom of our garden ran along the rear of Job's and led to a large brick workshop, the site of Mr French the carpenter. Sometimes he let us stand at his door inhaling the delicious scent of wood shavings and watching him use his plane to shape the coffins he made. We knew what they were but saw them merely as objects, more interested in Mr French varnishing the surfaces and screwing on the brass handles than in what these odd shaped boxes would later contain. We played marbles and constrained games of cricket and football in this narrow passage and must have made an irritating row at times. Once Mr French ran out of his workshop shouting and swearing at us before throwing an axe in our direction. It didn't quite carry, landing in the dirt near my sandaled feet. Did he just hate making those death boxes? Had we done other awful things to bait him that I no longer remember? Quite possibly. It is the axe that stuck in the memory if, fortunately, nowhere else.

On the other side of this alley was the back door to 9 Longworth Road where Mr and Mrs Day lived. They were active in the chief local service industry, taking in lodgers. Mr Day was a policeman "and did a lot of night duty," according to my parents. When they spoke of Mrs Day it was evident that she was someone who would not be invited for tea. For a start, she put up actors from the Oxford Playhouse. This might have been glamourous but in some way that I couldn't grasp it implied behaviour that did not take place in our house. John Gordon Ash, director at the Playhouse, lodged there and was thought to be a very close friend of Mrs Day. Mr Day was fair haired as was Mrs Day, so when a few years later she gave birth to a dark haired and dark-complexioned baby Mrs Day felt compelled to volunteer an explanation. "I drank such a lot coffee while I was expecting. You've no idea." Some neighbours did.

Their daughter Elaine was a year older than me. We didn't play together because she was a girl. My mother gave me a telling off when she overheard Jeremy Taylor and me saying that if we could catch Elaine we would strip her. "Strip" was to us an incredibly naughty word. We had no thought of actually carrying out the threat and in any case there was no need. Jeremy had a sister and reported all we needed to know: "It's like a little bum at the front."

On the opposite corner of Longworth Road from Job's was Jago's corner shop, standby for emergencies. It was the source of occasional treats on a summer evening when it was too light and too warm to get to sleep. Dad would go across the road for ice cream and a bottle of lemonade so we could have ice cream sodas. A more regular source of treats was Blencowes bread and cake shop just past Auntie Florey's house. I often went for a penny halfpenny current bun, an iced bun, a fatty cake or best of all a sticky Chelsea bun which could be unwound and eaten from the end finishing with the soft spongy core. Down the side of the shop was the usually open door to the bakery where we could watch the dough being made and stirred. The bakers liked to show off in front of us kids.

"Bit of extra flavour George?" asked one.

"Yea, give it some," was the reply, whereupon the first heaved up a great mouthful of phlegm and gobbed it into the mix.

"That should do it."

It never crossed our minds to stop buying the buns.

Shopping was nearly all done down the Kingston Road and Walton Street. Griffiths the paper shop delivered our *Daily Express* and supplied me with comics. Here I learned an important lesson about grown-ups: they did not necessarily know more than you. This was a breakthrough in those deferential and obedient times. Dad sent me to buy some carbon paper for him, ten inches by eight. I asked for it from the woman in the shop whom I knew well. She went off to find some and returned looking apologetic.

"Sorry", she said, "We've only got carbon paper in eight by ten."

I had to think for a moment and asked,

"Wouldn't it be the same if you turned it on its side?"

She looked puzzled and went off to fetch a packet of the eight by ten and turned it round in her hands.

"Aah, yes."

I had my haircuts at Mr Taylor's barber's shop in Walton Street. He wore a green overall and his own hair was impressively plastered with brilliantine. You didn't make an appointment but just turned up and waited your turn on one of the chairs against the wall. All too often a grown-up would come in claiming to be in a hurry and Mr Taylor would say, not ask, "Alan you don't mind waiting while I do Mr Brett?" So I waited. There would be a lot of manly talk about the price of things or Oxford City football team. The cut itself did not take long. An important part of it was a lot of rhythmic scissor clipping away from the head before each attack on the hair. Snip, snip, snip, snip, snip, cut. It emphasised the technicality, even the artistry, of what Mr Taylor was accomplishing. He showed me the end results with a flourish of the hand mirror. I would never have dreamed of saying anything but, "Thank you."

Nearby was Cape's the drapers on the corner of Juxon Street, a larger shop than most. It was quiet inside, more what Mum would have called "select" or even "refined". She would go there for buttons, ribbons, material; it was a place of textures and colours and the promise of the special, a little luxury even. I remember once making our way along Walton Street in a dense, deliciously exciting, green-grey fog. There were several such in my childhood when you could only just make out the other side of the street. They were mysterious and a little frightening.

On the opposite side of the street was Burbank's the chemist, a regular stopping place. I don't recall my needing much medication or any pills but there were some regulars, pink cough mixture and vapour chest rub in the winter and always large jars of cod liver oil and malt. This was a delicious sweet, glutinous brown stuff, a daily spoonful of which Mum said would make me "grow up strong," or as Dad would have it, "put hairs on your chest". There must have been a fishy flavour but I only remember the satisfying sweetness and the treacly stickiness that made whirls on the spoon and created a long, fascinating tendril as you lifted it from the jar. You could then either twist the spoon round and round to wind in the tendril or, better, hold the spoon high and lower the thin sticky filament onto your tongue. Sometimes Mum would send me on a mysterious errand to Burbank's with a note in an envelope. The covert nature of the mission told me that the package I returned with was something to do with her being a woman.

I would go with Mum, and later be sent, to the Co-op further up Walton Street. This was fun. It had different counters for different groceries and a separate cashier's booth. You gave your magic share number, the assistant put your money and the bill in a little container which she fixed to an overhead wire. She pulled a wooden handle propelling the container across the shop to the cashier with an exciting whizzing sound to the cashier's booth. Back came the change and the receipt.

The Co-op and Mr Knight's, the greengrocers next door, were at the extremities of our regular beat. Many foods were rationed and could only be purchased with a coupon from your ration book. We were registered with Cleaver's Quality House at the near end of Walton Street - it's a Londis now - and where your ration books were registered was where you purchased staples like tea, butter, margarine, lard, bacon, cheese, biscuits and jam. It was quite a ritual as the relevant coupon was carefully clipped from the ration book, allowing you to buy your three ounces of bacon or four ounces of margarine for that week.

Rations were actually smaller after the war ended in 1945 than during it but we had a supplementary and clandestine source of protein. Mum's great friend from when she was a servant was Auntie Anne, who had married Range Clarke and lived on their farm in Oakley a few miles north-east of Oxford. Once Dad had bought his first motor, an army surplus Austin pick up, we could drive over to visit and return with booty. Fresh eggs were a prize as they were in short supply. Like most people we made scrambled eggs with tinned dried egg powder. Mum believed that many foods contained a magic ingredient known as "goodness". Eggs were one of these and it gave her huge satisfaction to sit her little boy down in front of a boiled egg and bread and butter soldiers. This, she knew, was what the best mothers did. In time I went off soft eggs and stayed off. Mum liked to say that this was because I had had so many when I was small, a comfort to her that she had done her duty and more.

There were other prizes from Oakley, among them an occasional chicken, a luxury at that time. I was thrilled watching Range stalk the selected bird round the farm yard, grab it and with a mighty twist crack its neck. Did he then put it down and watch as it ran around or have I imagined that? I have not imagined the posthumous flapping when he held it up by the legs. Mum plucked it at home. I think that the feathers, evidence of backdoor purchasing, were disposed of furtively. Yet I used to retain one or two long ones to stick in my hair so I could be a Red Indian. Best of all from the Oakley farm was "The New Look". This was the code name (after Christian Dior's revolutionary long skirts and tiny waists collection of 1947) adopted for our black market half a salt pig which hung on the back of the kitchen door. The scale of this haul had the glamour of a pools win.

Sunday dinner at one o'clock was the highlight of the week. I heard many stories of the competition to get hold of a joint of meat. Mum asked for one at the butchers to be told that she couldn't have it as "That's for Mrs So and So." Dad went to the shop to complain and a few days later the butcher brought a joint to our door. Another butcher would gravely inform customers that he hadn't had any lamb for months even when some was inexpertly hidden behind the counter. Happily, my parents found a new source, the Co-op butchers, where they knew the woman who took over there. Sometimes there was beef, source of the favourite Monday morning breakfast, dripping toast. Dripping, and especially the dark cold gravy poured over it, was a further source of that mysterious "goodness". Mum always baked a cake on Sunday afternoon, a custom from her early village life when the family would bake then to make use of the already hot coal fuelled oven. We had a gas oven but the Sunday old rhythm lingered on.

My favourite was a ginger cake, preferably soft in the middle and eaten when still warm.

It was a tight little family world. Was there a Kingston Road community? I don't remember it like that. We knew the shopkeepers and some neighbours but I don't think there was much popping in and out of each other's houses. If we were having new potatoes of a Sunday, I would be sent across the road to Mr and Mrs Honey for some mint from their garden. There was the kindly Miss Florey. When we had fresh eggs from Oakley I was deputed to take a couple to one of Mum's customers Miss Fathers. She was a friendly soul who lived on the corner of Plantation Road and baby sat me when I was small. She sat, heavily wrapped up, in a ground floor room thick with the smell of mustiness and sweat, what I took to be the smell of old age. Mum had a friend up the road she went to the pictures with on a Wednesday. There were one or two we didn't get on with, "her and her click", as Mum would put it. Probably "common as muck".

Otherwise it was us. And we were to comprise a fourth. My parents who had waited six years before I was born were expecting a second child five years after me. They were prudent. You had what you could afford whether that be furniture, outings or children. I liked the idea of a younger brother or sister. I envisioned myself passing the new one in its pram and giving it a wink in an "I'm a grown up" way. Adults did a lot of winking at children in those days. It was meant as a kindly greeting, sharing mischief or just instead of knowing what to say to a child. Anyway, I would certainly be winking at my young sibling. Dad had booked a place for Mum in a private ward at the maternity home in Walton Street only to be told by the receptionist that there was no bed when the time came. This was another little battle for Dad. He wasn't having that.

He'd given nearly eight months' notice. Either his place was being usurped or people must have booked before they were pregnant. The matron relented.

The winter of 1946-7 was one of the coldest on record. There were huge snow falls and in Oxford the temperature did not rise above freezing for nearly two weeks. The conditions were made worse by power cuts and shortage of fuel. Into this on 25 February came my baby brother. I remember trudging through the piled snow to visit. My parents decided to call him David and said that he could have a second name which I could choose. I opted for John. Now there were four of us to be fed and clothed. This was our community.

Wyatt family 1913. Patriarch in his pomp. L to R. Back: Gladys, George, Frank, Roberta, Percy. Centre: Gertrude, Maud, William (grandfather), Ada (grandmother), Bill. Front: Lucy, Ron, Monica, Basil (Dad), Reg.

3
THE WYATTS

Our small family was established in North Oxford but the adopted territory of the greater Wyatts was East Oxford. My grandfather, William, was born in Burdrop, part of the pretty village of Sibford Gower in north Oxfordshire. He was the youngest of eight from a family that had worked as labourers on farms in the area of the Oxfordshire, Warwickshire and Gloucestershire borders. There were siblings born in all three counties. His only brother worked as a stableman and agricultural labourer. Sister Elizabeth, known as Bess, planned to emigrate, changed her mind and became a ladies' maid, travelled and in later life returned to Sibford to work as a dressmaker and run the village shop; another sister married a decorator and moved to London; one remained in the village, never married and was a coal dealer before partnering her elder sister in the shop and one died an infant. The other sister married a Burdrop man, a bricklayer, and moved with him to Oxford. They lived in Charles Street between the Iffley and Cowley Roads, an inner suburb growing rapidly, albeit piecemeal, in the last decades of the nineteenth century.

William arrived there as a seventeen-year-old bricklayer to lodge with them. It was a neighbourhood he never left. He was to bring up his family in eleven different houses on or off Cowley Road, all of them rented from his employer, Organ Brothers. Six of his seven sons worked "on the building" at one time or another, all of them for Bill Organ, referred to as "the Master". Construction was booming in the city as the population expanded rapidly, the motor industry developed and the university built extensively.

The townie Wyatt family's links to the university that made Oxford renowned were thin but catered for three basic needs. The bricklaying father and brothers worked on college or university buildings, putting a roof over academic heads. Then, for a brief period in later years my grandmother took in and fed one or two undergraduate lodgers, not just roof but food in the mouth. Thirdly, two of my aunts provided more intimate comfort to the young men of the university, namely sex.

My father was born in Rose Cottage, lately Powell Ltd. timber merchants, on Cowley Road, nearly opposite Cowley Marsh in what was then an open area of fields and cricket grounds between the city and Cowley village. He was the youngest of thirteen, two others died in infancy. At birth he weighed a mere three and a half pounds so the vicar was hastily summoned for a christening. His parents had not yet thought of a name so they gave him the vicar's name, Basil.

I have few memories of my grandfather. I don't think he ever came to our house. Very occasionally we went to visit him at 203 Cowley Road, next door to Organ's offices, and hard by the Oxford Workhouse. I was small; he was large, bald and with a thick moustache and I sensed I was in the presence of greatness. He would take his false teeth out and smack his lips and gums together to amuse me. Then I would sit quietly in the twilight as the elders chatted in a desultory manner. I couldn't understand this. Why don't they put the lights on? But they liked the enfolding tranquillity of the gloom and then it was time to go.

My grandfather died when I was nine and I was not taken to the funeral, not thought proper for a child I suppose. He was an Edwardian patriarchal figure. There's a photograph of him, a potentate surrounded by his wife and thirteen children, the little ones at the front with arms folded like a football team. This is the Tory working class in its pomp. The household revolved round him. There was his chair in which he liked to read the newspaper and in which on one else was allowed to sit. When he wanted another cup of tea he let people know by throwing his slops into the sink. He had a dog, Tiger, a bull terrier whippet cross. He played the cornet in the Oxford silver band. In later years, he had a Sunday ritual, first sitting in the front room window to watch his old workmates going to the pub at twelve o'clock. Then after his dinner he was back at two o'clock to see them weaving their ways home the worse for wear, "up the loop" as he put it. In the evening, he walked down to the cathedral in Christ Church to hear the choir, on parade in his best suit and trilby hat, carrying a walking stick.

It had been my dad's job to take the best suit to the pawn shop in Brewer Street, off St Aldates. This was a fair way off but the woman next door used the nearer Cowley pawn shop so that was ruled out. Did they hope she wouldn't know? Dad took the suit down on Monday morning and picked it up on Saturday for his father to wear at the weekend. "It wasn't much of a way to go on," Dad said, "because you were always one week behind with your housekeeping but I don't suppose my mother knew any other way really." I think William was something of a tyrant but his children respected him for two great virtues which were by no means universal at the time, "he never went boozing and he always provided." Each week he kept sixpence back from his wages so that on a Thursday his wife, Ada, could say, "Have you got that sixpence, Will? Give it here." Sixpenny worth of stewing steak would feed them all.

He had left school at eleven and his eldest sister had paid for his apprenticeship. He was a hard and skilled worker, a clever foreman who could lay out any kind of building without error and a demanding man to work for. His sons pressed him as to why he had never set up on his own. His answer was that with so many children and with the family homes rented from his employer, the risk was too great. Like all leaders of a herd he had to defend his position. Many sons were taken on to work under their fathers in the building trades. Sooner or later the bosses would make the young ones foremen and fathers found themselves working under their sons. My grandfather did not intend to allow this to happen to him. He was nearly eased out at Organs by his son Frank and once he had seen off that challenge was careful to hoard his technical knowledge. When Dad came to work under him he was never shown the plans in the site office so he could not develop into a threat. Frank followed the same practise: the plans were his alone.

My grandmother Ada died in 1938 before I was born. She was a good looking woman, the eldest of the ten children of, according to Wyatt lore, the "prettiest family in Stanton St John". This was the Matthews, with their black curly hair and grey eyes. Her father had kept a pub and was a boozer. Ada was in service before marrying at 22. I was told that she suffered from nervous trouble and went regularly to pub with her sister. Small wonder, as she had fifteen pregnancies in nineteen years, moved house every four or five years and when my father was small had eleven children living at home. Dad remembered the morning routine, waiting upstairs until his mother called, "All dress, all dress". This gave her and his elder sisters time to cut the pieces of bread and marge or bread and sugar for breakfast.

They all washed in the sink and had a weekly scrub in a galvanised tin bath in the kitchen with hot water from a brick copper, boys one night, girls the next. They had no tooth brushes and no pants, vests or pyjamas. Clothes were hand me downs and shoes were mended with paper and cardboard to cover the holes and keep feet dry. When the uppers came away from the soles the children bored holes with a meat skewer and tied them together with string.

The strain on Ada broke out often on Sunday lunchtimes. There was sometimes rabbit which my grandfather bred when they had a garage attached to one of their houses. With only a small range and oven she couldn't cook everything at home so the children had to take potatoes up to the bake house in Hertford Street and pick them up at one when they were ready. Then the children would squabble at the table and poor Ada, with four sons in the army during the First World War, would break down in tears and leave the dinner table saying that she would do away with herself. This frightened Dad and the other small ones.

The three youngest boys all had jobs, the money from which went to Ada to help with the keep. Dad was an errand boy at Twinings on Cowley Road, Reg, two years older, had a paper round and Ron, two years older again, cleaned shoes at houses in Divinity Road before school. The latter was always "Bread and Marge Avenue" to the Wyatts who considered that the people who lived there were putting on airs and graces but skimped on their grub. When the family moved from Cricket Road, where the woman next door had a pint of stout for her elevenses, to a larger house in Leopold Street, Ada made the children walk round there in ones and twos at intervals to disguise from the new neighbours how many there were. The family was short of furniture for these larger premises and Ada ordered a new carpet and a three-piece suite for the front room. Only a few weeks later Dad found her crying in that room. She had been unable to keep up the payments and the furniture had been taken away. Later, she put money down on a piano although no one in the house could play and that, too, was soon reclaimed. It must have all become too much for Ada at one time for she and my dad, her youngest, went to stay in a little cottage in Stanton St John with one of her sisters and her children. William cycled over at weekends.

For all Ada's difficulties with money Christmas seems to have stood out as a time of warmth, comfort and wellbeing. William formed a group with three other members of the Oxford City Brass

Band and they went round the streets and pubs playing carols of an evening. This brought in enough money for there to be a turkey, a York ham and a few presents for the little ones.

There were eighteen years between my grandmother's eldest child, Gertrude, and my father, which explains in part why we didn't see a lot of his family when I was a boy. I had more than 22 Wyatt cousins in Oxford, most of whom I never met. Another reason was that my mother didn't think much of the Wyatts.

Gert, the eldest, was in service and, when my father was only four, got married. I met her only a few times, a strong looking woman with a large head and full Wyatt nose. (The thick Wyatt nose may have come from Dad's grandmother who was said to have been so ugly that her husband had to be paid to marry her.) As a boy Dad had stayed with Gert and went round on her husband's cart. He was Fred Passey, a rag and bone trader and a knacker man, selling horsemeat for hounds.

Roberta, Berta, the next eldest emigrated to Canada when she was 21, settling in Windsor, Ontario and married Reg Millin who worked in the Ford Motor plant. In later years, they came over several times trailing a faint aura of transatlantic glamour, faint because it was Canada not the USA, glamour because they had done well enough to cross the Atlantic every few years.

Next was Uncle Billy, christened I now learn as Cecil William. Where the Cecil came from I cannot imagine but he certainly behaved like a Cecil within the family. He was an office worker, first at Ducker's shoe shop in Turl Street, then as a wages clerk in the welfare department at Morris Motors. From all accounts, he thought this white collar work gave him a superior status among the Wyatts and sought special treatment. The family group photo shows him in round spectacles with hair plastered down and divided in the middle. He served as a lance corporal in the Oxfordshire and Buckinghamshire Light Infantry during the First World War. As a boy, he had been a disciple of the Cowley Fathers, an Anglican religious order based in Marston Street, and had thoughts of becoming a priest. He played the clarinet well enough to be in Dr Hugh Allen's Oxford orchestra. I remember him as a smartly turned out fellow with a silver moustache married to his second wife Elizabeth, a piano teacher, considered "lah di dah" by his siblings and who, as my Dad put it, talked "poundnoteish". Bill was the only one of the seven boys never to work on the building. He had aspirations for something different and in a modest way achieved them.

All Dad's brothers married. "Their girls were all plain," said Dad, "but came from good families." He added an afterthought, "So that was a step up." The all-important "step up". Frank, the tallest of the sons, followed his father as a foreman for Organs. He was an impulsive and self-confident tradesman, adept at deflecting blame when he made a mistake. He would order a carpenter to do something a certain way and when the architect arrived to say this was wrong, Frank would ball out the man for disobeying him. Like his mother, who enjoyed her tanner each way ("Got anything good for today, Ron?"), and like many of his siblings, Frank was a racing man. When the boss found his racing paper on site Frank would shout at the other workers that they should not leave their paper laying around like this. It can't have been too much of a problem, for old man Organ would disguise his voice and ring up Frank with phoney tips. I barely remember meeting Uncle Frank but he clearly had some dash and charisma. As a sergeant in the Royal Artillery in the First War he won the Military Medal for gallantry for saving a gun in the mud and then won a bar to it for another act of bravery. Frank worked for Organs all his life. When he was ill in hospital in later years, Bill Organ visited and gave him his cards.

George was also in France in that war as a corporal in the Hampshire Regiment. He was gassed and invalided out in October 1918. He worked on the counter at Sainsbury's in Oxford High Street and after the war for an insurance company. This came to an end when he was caught fiddling after which he had a spell as a building labourer. When his wife's parents died they sold their house and bought a general store on the Isle of Wight. I never knew him.

Another uncle I never met was Percy, referred to always as "Uncle Diddly". He may have been one of the reasons Mum was not so keen on her in-laws. He had delivered parcels "for a high class tailor", then served as a private in the Oxford and Bucks. He was in the bugle band and played The Last Post at Rose Hill War Memorial after the war. Percy was a good enough footballer to play for Oxford City, in its day a top amateur side, lured there from Cowley FC in return for a job in the transport department at Morris's.

In February 1355, a row over the quality of the beer served in an Oxford tavern had led to two days of armed fighting between students and townspeople. Nearly a hundred people died. If not on that scale, tension between the two worlds persisted. Percy played his part in the Wyatts' town versus gown story, sticking a lighted Woodbine in the ear of a passing undergrad (they were always "undergrads" or "varsity men" to townspeople, never "students") to initiate a fight. Dad used to scrap with them later. Percy worked as a brickie for Organs and then as a lorry driver, which is what he was doing in 1938 when convicted of receiving stolen goods, tyres and vehicle parts, from Morris's Cowley factory, and sentenced to six months in prison.

Percy also conducted one of the racing fiddles that the family specialised in. There were no betting shops then and bookmakers legal and otherwise handled many postal bets in their office as well as (illegally) collecting slips from pubs and workplaces. Percy would post letters to himself with a lightly written pencil address and the flap not stuck down. When he received it the following day he would write out a bet on one of the afternoon's winners, seal the envelope, readdress it this time in ink, and slip it under the bookie's door next morning along with the rest of the post. The postmark was from the day before the race and the bet apparently valid. This couldn't last and the scam ended when got his timing wrong one morning and was caught delivering his envelope well after the postman had called.

Ron, who was close in age to Dad, also had a cunning swindle with a friend. They worked out a code of tunes, each one standing for a number between one and sixteen. The friend would wander into the bookie's office with the amount of his bet, the time and place of the race already written out but not the number of the horse. Bookmakers had no live commentary and there was a delay between the finish of the race and the result reaching the bookie. The friend would engage the bookie in a chat to distract him while Ron used a phone box to get the quickest possible result from the course. He then walked past the bookmaker's window whistling the tune for the number of the winning horse. His friend would say, "I'd better get on with it," add the number to his betting slip and pass it over. Ron grinned like a lad with an extra portion of ice cream as he described this to me.

Ron was a dapper, affable fellow. Like the others, he left school at thirteen and was an errand boy before learning to be a brickie He was a very good one, according to Dad, "But he did the work too cheaply, thought it clever to work faster than the others. Like my Dad and Frank, he worked too hard for somebody else." As a young man Ron had emigrated to Canada but returned after a year. He later left the building trade and bought a village bakery, never having been in one before. Later, he and his wife moved to Devon to run a guesthouse where we did visit them. He and Dad became as close as two Wyatts ever did get in later years.

Dad's sisters were all chatterboxes, entertaining whenever I saw them as a boy. Maud had a wide face and Wyatt nose. She did well at school and was asked to stay on as a pupil teacher but her mother needed her to start earning. She worked in shops on Cowley Road and in a newsagent in Abingdon; "I just saw the job and applied for it," she told me as if describing a bold move to the South Seas. She took her step up in marrying Harold Martyr. His family kept a "high class hairdressers" in Cornmarket and Harold served as an officer in the Gurkhas before working as a survey officer for the Post Office. His brother was a vicar and, as Maud put it to me, "They were a churchy lot. Just the opposite of the Wyatts, rough and ready."

I liked Auntie Lucy best. She never stopped talking and buoyed one up. Lucy had always been very kind to my mother and she and her husband Arthur kept the stores at Florence Park, Iffley, a source of a few extra rations during the war. This continued though my parents were careful not to seem too greedy by going to tea too often. A Sunday afternoon visit took me through the exciting silence of the darkened shop and even more eye-poppingly through the storeroom, where stood boxes of cornflakes, jams, sweets and chocolate in undreamed of abundance. Sweets were still rationed till 1953. We always came away with a few rashers of bacon, some butter or a couple of bars of Fry's Mint Crème.

Auntie Glad liked to be called Auntie Pat, or "Auntie Pet", as my parents would say, emphasising what they considered an affectation. She was the one who stayed home to look after her parents after a flighty youth. "She and Monica were both a bit of a goer in their day," said Maud, "they had rather a fluffy name, going to all the dances picking up boys." They went out with undergrads "who had money and could give a girl a good time". This was a source of anguish for their mother who would wait up and shout, trying to hit them when they came in. "She knew what was going on," my father said, "there was no pill in those days." An uncle on my mother's side called them a pair of "bloody prostitutes". I suspect he meant no more than they were putting it about, but I believed it literally when in my teens. Monica worked in a flower shop in the covered market and in Week's cake shop in Cornmarket before a job in a pub in Kidlington, "for some man she got in touch with," as Maud put it with heavy emphasis. Eventually, in her forties, Monica married a quiet solicitor and moved away from Oxford.

Closest in age to Dad was Reg, another bricklayer at Organs who worked at Morris's during the Second World War. He lived in a council house in Cowley with a sizeable garden in which he kept ducks, pigs, geese and chickens, many of which, according to Dad, had the run of the house. During rationing he slaughtered pigs at home and cut them up on the kitchen table. One of his sons once found a dead pig in the bath. Reg, often in trouble with the police, had a lurcher and he was often off poaching. He also sold logs from a lorry. In the late forties petrol was still rationed, with greater allowances for commercial vehicles than for private motoring. Late one evening Reg, who was fond of Basil, turned up at 15 Kingston Road to warn him that the police might call on him and if they did to say that he, Reg, had been round to see about a delivery of logs. His lorry had been spotted outside the Three Horseshoes pub and they were after him for using a commercial vehicle for private travel. Dad's response was, "There are thirteen of us, why pick on me?"

An hour after Reg had left the police duly arrived asking if Dad had seen his brother that evening. Dad gave a typical Wyatt response: "What if I have?" Petrol offences were taken very seriously especially, I would guess, if the culprit was someone police regularly had in their sights. Reg was charged with "misuse of petrol" and Dad subpoenaed as a witness. When he got to the court Reg moved into action, "Look, Bas, I'll tell you what you should say", adding, "I didn't actually deliver any logs but came to see if you might like some." I presume Dad played his part, for Ron was acquitted.

In 1988 a book of photographs of Oxford was published. It included a photo of the rear of a house in Marshall Road in the 1950s. Strewn over the garden were a couple of horse carts, bits of fencing, some timber, chickens, a bicycle, and other oddments, together with washing on the line. Below was a photo of the occupants, an artful looking man with bag tie on his trousers and a snappy trilby tilted on his head. He stares at the camera, giving nothing away in his expression, while alongside him are his two knowing boys in short trousers. I was sure that this was Reg and two of his sons and showed it to Dad. He agreed but later denied it, embarrassed, I think, by the rag-tag appearance of both house and the figures. But it was Reg, as Dad subsequently admitted, and those knowing-looking two boys in the picture did know something. Both they and a third brother worked for Organs. The proprietor sent his own son to public school but had little faith in him, so when old man Organ retired from the business it was two young Wyatt brothers who bought it and prospered, developing a sports centre and a golf course. So, Wyatt boys, nearly all of whom had worked for Bill Organ and whose homes had been owned by him, succeeded in eventually stepping up and over their former "Master".

And then there was Dad.

Working for Organs - Dad on right with plans for once, brother Frank centre rear.

4
LAYING A PRETTY BRICK

Parents bring up children in the long shadow cast by their own childhood, seeking to replicate or reinforce the good, avoid or improve on the bad. I think my father sought to emulate the security he felt his parents had given him. His father had always been in work and even if he had cut a lordly figure in the household, he did offer the top of his boiled egg to his youngest as a treat. On a summer Sunday he would take Dad, Ron and Reg swimming at Long Bridges, an open-air bathing place on a backwater of the Thames. William rode his bike, the boys running alongside. Dad's mother was a fragile figure at times but provided essential maternal warmth. It was when her children were grown up that she would slip off to The Prince of Wales pub on the corner of Temple Street with her sister or friends.

There had certainly been poverty when the children were all at home but with the elder ones at work and bringing in money life had improved. When his older brothers brought their girls home to tea there was cake and Dad was allowed a piece but knew to say "No, thank you," when offered a second. Ada took in two "varsity men" at the four-storey house on the corner of Rectory Road and cooked their evening meal. They paid at the end of term and it was then that Ada, dazzled by the unfamiliar sum of cash, paid the deposit on the unplayed piano that was soon returned.

Dad saw hard work and education as a route to better things for his own family. He applied himself to the former and when Mr Gray offered an access all areas pass for his elder son, he took it. His own education had been limited. He attended East Oxford Council School - "the headmaster was an MA"- but for one crucial year went every morning to a special school to help his bad stammer and consequently missed many important English and arithmetic lessons. The stammer did improve but never entirely disappeared. He played football for the school in a proper football jersey but wearing his ordinary shoes and short trousers and had trials for Oxford Boys at both football and cricket without success. He did swim for the school, hiring another much bigger boy's bathing costume which had to be pinned up to stay on.

Soon after leaving school at fourteen he found a job at the *Oxford Chronicle* newspaper in the High Street. The *Chronicle* had been founded in 1837 and lasted until 1927, when it merged with the *Oxford Times*. He was one of three boys on the payroll. Their jobs included cutting out small ads from other local papers so they could target the same people for ads in the *Chronicle*. They were lads and larked about in the room devoted to stacked back numbers by throwing the neatly folded papers at each other, creating havoc. Dad was serious enough about this first job to go to night school for two terms to learn shorthand with hopes of becoming a reporter. On his walk to work down Cowley Road and over Magdalen Bridge he used to meet some girls on their way to school and began seeing one of them on Saturday afternoons. The budding romance ended suddenly when it turned out that her father was manager of the pawn shop where Dad had taken his father's suit. Between pawnbroker and customer was a gulf that could not be crossed.

The call of the building site was a summons the Wyatt boys could not deny. After three years at the *Chronicle*, Dad went in his week's summer holiday to see his father and brothers working in Cowley. It was a sunny August day and everyone on the job was laughing and joking. The open air, cheerful mates, this looked like enjoyable work so he light-heartedly asked his father when he could be part of all this. Wyatt senior seized the chance to welcome his youngest into the family trade sent him to see Bill Organ, "the Master" as he was called, who said he could start straightaway. Dad only went back to the *Chronicle* to give his notice. Here was another Wyatt brickie in the making, the fifth brother to join their father on Organ's books. He was small for seventeen but the manual labour soon filled him out. That first week he worked 54 ½ hours and netted nine shillings and five pence. His father was the top paid foreman on Organs' books, two and six an hour.

It was very hard work. There was a check board outside the foreman's office and each man hung his number on it as he arrived for work. The board was taken in two minutes past seven thirty after which you were docked half an hour's pay. Men went from site to site asking, "Any chance of a start, guv'nor?" Organs, Dad claimed, worked longer hours than other firms. They would carry on in the rain and he was often soaking wet before his father, not wanting the gang to lose too much time, would blow to halt work. If you were not working for whatever reason you were not paid. One year when he was still an apprentice prolonged frost shut down jobs for two months. Sometimes they started at six thirty and had breakfast on the job, bread and jam for most but his father had a labourer cook him a bloater or fried egg. The lunch break, mid-morning, was ten minutes, dinner break at midday was half an hour and later a fifteen-minute stop for tea.

Dad enjoyed the camaraderie and liked the little song, "We bricklayers lead a jolly good life and we calls for nut brown ale". He began earning sixpence an hour and added to it by clearing snow in the winter and "scouting", acting as a ball boy, for the undergrads playing tennis on the Iffley Road courts in the summer. In time, he had another Wyatt way to add to his earnings, partly to make up for money lost on late night card games played in secret in his parents' house. Dad's friend Aubrey Cooke used to collect bets for his father who operated as a bookmaker. Aubrey picked them up from offices and building sites; his father collected them from the pubs in East

Oxford at lunchtime, after which he would go home and fall asleep for an hour or two. Aubrey bought the early afternoon edition of the newspaper which carried the winners of the first three races in the stop press. Then he would write out a bet on a couple of the winners in Dad's name and slip it into the sleeping man's satchel. When his father woke up Aubrey would say that he thought his friend had a winning bet and wanted the money so he could go out dancing. Cooke senior would search in his bag and, sure enough, there was a winning bet. Aubrey and Dad split the proceeds.

Dad enjoyed bricklaying from the start and continued to do so until nearly eighty. A Wyatt boy liked the accolade, "he can lay a pretty brick." After four years he asked for full rate and was in effect qualified, for he had signed no apprenticeship document. He had spells with other firms, Benfield and Loxley – still based in Cowley - and Kingerlee. He worked on Milham Ford School, Barclays Bank, Headington, the Royal Oxford Hotel, the Churchill Hospital and the chapel and residential buildings of Lady Margaret Hall. Large contracts like these provided six months or more employment for a bricklayer, a single house only about four weeks. All labour was on one hour's notice. On a Thursday the foreman went round the site, "You, you and you, you're finished tonight," and that was that.

Dad preferred these other employers to Organs where he felt he was held back. His father had taught him bricklaying but no more. If he popped down from the scaffolding to check something on the plans in the office his father, protecting his hegemony, would follow him down. "Now, back up there, my son, and get on with your work." When Dad worked under other foremen at Organs they saw him as the son of a rival and kept him only as long as they absolutely had to, protective of their own ways of running a job. Still, he was never out of work for long and had money in his pocket.

He became a bit of a lad about town. When he bought his brother Bill's Humber motor bike, paying a little each week, his friend Gilbert Kimber also bought a second-hand motor bike and the pair relished the popularity that came with their own transport. They bought suits from the Fifty Shilling Tailors, a menswear chain which offered a made to measure suit for two pounds ten, about £115 today. They opted for the seventy-five-shilling superior version, say £ 170. "It was all show," said Dad. "I had no decent underwear - pants, vests or pyjamas." The two of them were returning from a dance in Abingdon one Saturday when Kimber's front tyre blew out, crashing him to the ground and knocking him out. When he regained consciousness, Dad put him on the back of his bike to take him to hospital. Kimber asked where they were going and Dad told him. "No," said Kimber, "I don't want to go to hospital. I've got holes in my pants. Take me home and stay with me, Bas." Which he did.

Dad was put on a job in Cheltenham, where he would stay through the week, and he began courting the landlord's daughter. This continued for a few months after he moved back to Oxford. He went over at weekends and brought her to his home a few times. "She was a nice, refined girl," he recalled, "much too good for me. When I went over there on a Saturday we'd be in the sitting room where she and her younger sister would play the piano to me. A fair bit different to what I was used to on a Saturday night." Eventually he found it all a bit quiet for him and a long way to go; the romance fizzled out. It was, perhaps, a step up too far.

Dancing, drinking and fighting were his more usual Saturday entertainments. Once, he and Kimber were in a brawl with some soldiers who were causing trouble at a dance in Cheltenham. At the end of the evening the manager warned them that a gang of the soldiers were waiting outside to give them a going over and helped them slip out of a back way to escape. A basement hall near the Elm Tree pub, on the corner of Jeune Street and Cowley Road, hosted a Saturday dance that usually ended in a free for all. "No knives or kicking or any of that," said Dad, "you just had a fair sort of set-to." One evening, he, Kimber and another friend Harold Lisemore returned from a dance at the Clarendon Press in Walton Street. As they walked along Beaumont Street, Lisemore spotted four undergrads. He took off his cap and, adopting a suitably humble tone, went up to them asking if they could help an out of work bricklayer. They gave him a few coppers so Kimber thought he would try the same trick when they encountered three more students crossing Magdalen Bridge. "Please Sir, spare a penny for a poor bricklayer," pleaded Kimber. One of the undergrads snatched the proffered cap and threw it into the Cherwell and a fight broke out. Kimber jumped on the back of one of the undergrads, arms around his neck. Lisemore aimed a punch at the student who swung round so the blow missed its target only to hit the desperately clinging Kimber full in the face. The parties separated.

No one ever seemed to get seriously hurt or run in by the police, save for an occasion when Dad and a few mates were caught peeing in the street. They were marched down the station where the sergeant lined them up and explained that they could all be charged with indecency, a charge which would be a disgrace and cause major trouble for them, or the matter could be sorted out there and then. They opted for the latter, whereupon the sergeant went down the line punching each of them in the face in turn.

It wasn't all work, pubbing and fighting. Pubbing no doubt brought the Oxford City darts league medal that he won, but Dad played a lot of football, winning a handful of league and cup medals in Oxfordshire with the East Oxford Corinthians and others. He looked back at this time with some resignation. "My youth wasn't much to be proud of. I think my stammer was part of the trouble. When I'd had a drink with the boys I felt more confident. With girls, I was more conscious of my stammer." He was fit, a good craftsman and in work but spent all his money every week, that was "Until I met Hettie, who put me on the right track for a better, more useful life."

They met in East Avenue early in 1935. Hettie Hooper had a lovely soft, fair complexion, a thin strong nose and a lively expression. She was a couple of inches over five feet tall and always dressed fashionably. Basil was five feet eight, had very dark hair, a thin pencil moustache and was thought a bit of a catch at the East Oxford dances. He had a thick Wyatt nose and an expression which could be cheeky and challenging one minute, pleading the next. Basil would be returning home at about five thirty as Hettie was setting out from where she lodged with her brother and sister in law to go to work at Twinings Wine Lounge in Cornmarket. After several encounters, he plucked up the courage to ask her out and they went to the cinema on her evening off. Hettie had her expectations. On the third or so such outing they walked to the Cowley Road Picture Palace where Basil joined the queue but she walked onwards to the bus stop. Basil trotted after her to find out what was wrong. "Well, after spending ages getting ready I'm not always going to the Cowley Road pictures. I want to go somewhere else: into town." They did.

They were an Oxford courting couple. One summer evening Basil punted from Magdalen Bridge to the Cherwell pub in Summertown and back, more than two miles each way, after bricklaying all day. It was too far; there was a tiff. But they were going strong. He took her home to tea with his parents, brother Bill and Gladys and Monica. They all liked her.

Basil's ways were changing and it was Hettie who was changing them. Dad's fellow roisterer, Kimber, was to be married. In Hettie's eyes, Kim was the man who had led her intended astray and she told him not to go to the wedding. He obeyed. By now she had taken her shy and stammering young man to meet her family. It was an expedition. They travelled by bus, changing at Witney, to Leafield, the West Oxfordshire village in which she had been born. He liked her mother, Annie, "very ladylike but quiet". Her father he thought "a bit rough" - this from a Wyatt - and "he always had a lot to say."

Hettie took Basil into the front room for a true Hooper welcome. Either side of the fire sat Victor, sister Daisy's husband, and brother Stan. "This is my boyfriend, Basil," she announced. Vic looked up and said "Ow do?" and carried on reading the newspaper. Stan glanced over and said, "Ow do?" and went back to his paper. And that was that. The Hoopers were folk of few words. They mellowed and on a Sunday evening all would go to one of the two Leafield pubs, The George or The Fox, where the others would in turn offer Basil a sup from their pint pots. This was a way of being sociable without being able to afford to stand rounds. He took it as the sign that he was accepted.

1917 Leafield. From left,
Phyllis, Daisy, Hettie
(Mum) Hooper.

5
THE FIDDLY TOWNERS

The Wyatts were townies; the Hoopers, country people. As Hettie began to civilise Basil she measured herself as many women do by the standards and behaviour of her mother. Annie Hooper lived an impoverished life in an isolated village but her character rose above her circumstances. I was only five when she died at 73, just a few months after her husband. Although I can only have seen her a very few times I do retain a warm memory of her presence. She looks out from the few photographs with a round, strong, kindly face, with short hair and glasses. There is one of me as a baby on her knee as she sits in our garden at Kingston Road, smiling, apple cheeked. She was much referred to in my childhood and so remained a significant, if physically absent, influence.

Mum always spoke of her mother as "proper" and "a lady", known in the village for her kindness, "the best woman who ever drew breath." She was particularly good to a woman with some sort of mental illness whom Annie would visit to sit with and talk in a shed she had had specially built at the bottom of her garden. I have a neatly written letter from her to Mum following a visit soon after I was born. "I have been wondering about you this awful weather we are snowed in here. I hardly remember snowing so much. I wondered if you could keep warm - be very careful dear & don't get about too much. One soon gets laid up… We did have to wait a long time for the bus Saturday night. I expect our Daisy told you. Well dears no more for the present." It is signed with the touching formality of a well-schooled country girl not used to writing many letters: "so with best love I remain your affect. Mother, A. Hooper."

Later, when I was in my teens, there would talk at home of "the way young people are nowadays", of declining morals and loose behaviour. A regular refrain from Dad was how "in our day" people couldn't afford "all this carrying on" or "this one parent kind of a job," albeit that his brother Billy had fathered a child with a woman he didn't marry. The fact was that my grandmother Annie was herself the only child of an unmarried mother, Charlotte Shayler, who gave birth at 25 and lived in Leafield the rest of her life. There was the occasional hint that Annie's father had been a gentleman farmer. The name Teasdale was often mentioned knowingly but mystery fathers are rarely identified as navvies or pedlars. In these circumstances people prefer to believe their blood has a touch of the class brush.

Twenty-year-old Annie was herself five months pregnant when she married Frederick Ivo Hooper my grandfather. And there was plenty more of this to come in this family as in so many. Small wonder if you were living in a place like Leafield. It had long been a remote village and still felt that way when I was a child in the late forties. The other name for it was Field Town and Dad always referred to it as "Fiddly Town". It was high, more than 600 feet above sea level, the highest point in Oxfordshire before the county boundaries were changed in the seventies. Moreover, it was in the middle of what had been the ancient royal forest of Wychwood. In the mid-nineteenth century, more than half the men of the village earned their living from the forest in some way, as woodmen, hurdle makers, gamekeepers and the like. From the 1850s there were large clearances in the forest but Field Towners retained a reputation all their own. They were said to be "different from those of surrounding parishes, and to be dark, small, secretive, boastful and unfriendly…. To say of a man that he comes from Fieldtown is to say he's a wife beater." In 1858 one James Akerman wrote that Field Town was "a large primitive village in the very heart of the forest. The inhabitants have always been noted for their uncouth dialect." All the forest villages were distinguished from surrounding villages by their poverty, reliant as most of the menfolk were on casual labour: hay making and harvest in summer, coppicing and enclosing in winter. There was much stealing of wood and poaching. It was only in 1927 that drinking water was brought to the village. Until then villagers had to go with yoke and buckets to a spring in the forest or buy from the water cart.

Because of its isolation Leafield folk intermarried. Nearly everyone was related to many other villagers, a small number of surnames dominated. In 1851 a fifth of the population, 160 people, were Pratleys, along with 49 Holloways, 47 Eeles, 40 Shaylers and 28 Wiggins. Consequently, many villagers were known by nicknames. Mum used to talk about "Doodleum" Pratley and "Brucicer". She referred to one whole family as the "Bagarses".

Some 2,000 acres of the forest were cleared in the late 1850s creating seven farms, for which new buildings and stone walls were erected and in 1860 Leafield's first church, designed by Sir George Gilbert Scott, was consecrated. It was almost certainly this burst of development that drew my great grandfather, James Hooper, to the village from his birth place in Aldsworth, a dozen miles away in Gloucestershire. Mum always said he built stone walls and he probably did. He was a stone quarrier when he first came to Leafield, later a mason's labourer then a stone mason. He married one of the many Holloways, Charity, three days before their daughter was born in 1860. Charity already had a son. There were three more children of which my grandfather Frederick Ivo was the youngest. James must have made something of a mark in the village as in 1889 he was bailiff to the court leet of the lord of the manor, the only known member of the Hoopers or the Wyatts to hold any kind of public office.

Fred Hooper, my grandfather, lived the rest of his life in several cottages around the Green in Leafield. As with his wife, I was five when he died. I remember him only as a large important person in the same room. He was a big man with a hare lip and worked as a stone mason like his father. It was the building trade that provided on both sides of my family.

Fred Hooper owned the only two books I ever knew as belonging to the family. One was on phrenology, which was a popular interest in the nineteenth century. The other which I have still was *A Voyage in Space* by H. H. Turner, based on Turner's Christmas 1913 lectures at the Royal Institution, an explanation of astronomical instruments, the moon, the sun and stars. Whether Fred ever read it I cannot be sure. He was certainly interested in inventions. He kept old bicycles in his shed. Mum described how he worked on one of them, eventually producing it with a propeller he had fitted and with a pair of wings attached. He pushed it to the edge of the village, mounted and set off down Whitley Hill towards the forest in the hope of taking off. It did not but was the talk of the village. Thus, the first time an aeroplane was spotted flying over Leafield a number of villagers ran up Barry Hill Tump, the tree crowned barrow which commands the very top of the village, and shouted, "It's Mr 'ooper's flying bike! It's Mr 'ooper's flying bike!"

This was a favourite family tale. To the Hoopers' in-laws it was seen as proof that Fred in particular and Fiddly Town people in general were backward and ignorant folk to be ridiculed. To Mum and her siblings it was evidence that their father had a bit of something about him that might have flourished if not trapped in rural poverty. When Mum was a regular attender at Wolvercote Women's' Institute in the 1970s she returned excited one evening after hearing a talk on odd tales from local villages. The speaker had told of the famous flying bicycle of Leafield and the eccentric old fellow who invented it. Fred was no genius but something was going on in his head.

My grandmother Annie's feet were on the ground. She cut out trousers for the village and was paid in kind with vegetables. Like nearly all the country women in Leafield and around 2,000 women in the West Oxfordshire villages, she worked as a gloveress. They were outworkers for glove factories in Woodstock, Charlbury and Chipping Norton, stitching, often by candlelight or oil lamp, leather gloves for riders, coachmen and the well-to-do. The cut skins were fetched on foot or delivered by carrier's cart and the sewn gloves returned by the same means.

My childhood visits to Leafield were special Sunday afternoon expeditions. Once Dad had bought his army surplus van when I was about five we could drive the eighteen or so miles, arriving along dark roads through Wychwood Forest. We entered the village passing the handsome Victorian church at the eastern point of the large triangular village green, in the middle of which was Leafield's school. Our destination was a thirties semi-detached house on the south side of the green, opposite the school. It had been built by Mum's elder brother Walter for their parents and was now lived in by brothers, Stan and John. I was struck by the fact that the house had not a number but a name, Marlborough View, and from the garden one could see for miles to distant hills. These, I was solemnly told, were the Marlborough Downs. Had I been more curious,

I would have noted that none of the houses on the green had a number. For decades or even centuries, the address had been simply "The Green".

More interesting to me than the view was a model of Leafield Church made in concrete by an uncle. With the spire rising to about four feet, it stood proudly in the garden, testament to a Hooper brickie's skill. Most interesting of all were Uncle Stan's pair of shotguns standing propped against the wall to the side of the fireplace. I could touch and examine but not hold them. In winter, the cupboard under the stairs served as a game larder, stuffed with hanging pheasants, the booty from Stan's poaching.

Usually other members of the family were visiting and we would all go along the green to The George, the then favoured pub. It was a large old building with a garden from which I remember a view of a buttercup field. Once or twice we went over for Leafield Club, a fete cum small fair just after Whitsun. This had once featured parades, dinners and Morris dancing but I remember only a merry gathering, much looked forward to by my mother as family and old village friends would try to return for Club day.

Visits to Leafield prompted Mum's memories of her childhood. The family lived in Virginia Cottage, a small house on the Green, near the church. Some years back I was in Leafield and as we passed this cottage a woman came out. I asked if I could see inside and explained why. The interior was not unexpected, two small rooms, a narrow staircase and two small rooms above, but it was still hard to imagine how eight or nine people had lived in such a space, as millions had all over the country.

The young Hettie was often sent across the Green to stay with Granny Charlotte. She was "a great big woman" known as Charl Puggie and lived in a cottage next to the butcher's. At harvest time

Mum and her siblings went leazing, collecting ears of corn missed in the reaping. They put them together in sheaves to bring home. There were other errands and Mum, who was always of a nervous temperament, remembered her worries. When still tiny she was sent on her own to fetch potatoes from her father's allotment, having to make her way across the fields to the other side of the village down by the forest. She did not have to go alone to buy rabbit or venison from Waterman's Lodge, but the long walk took in a stretch where the forest grew thickly and threateningly on both sides of the road. "I used to try to stay up close to Daisy - she was tall - or whoever was with me. I was frightened always and used to hold on tight." A more welcome errand later was fetching the milk from a farm in Witney Lane. The walk was nowhere near the forest and had another attraction. "I used to like it when Joey Bowles was going too. There was never any speaking… I was too shy I expect. I wasn't the forward sort. All the girls were after Joey."

A highlight of the children's year was Palm Sunday. This was the one day of the year when villagers were allowed to walk in Wychwood Forest. Mum would tell how they each took with them a bottle containing a piece of liquorice and some brown sugar. This they topped up at springs in the wood so that as the day went on the liquorice water became more and more diluted. From the way Mum talked of it I understood that the day was a big adventure and the home-made drink its special signifier. Try as I might, I couldn't see what was so wonderful about liquorice in water. I tried it with a Barrett's Liquorice All Sort in a glass of water, confirming the heretical thoughts I never shared with my mother.

Mum's eldest sister was Gladys, a large warm, cuddly figure with a round face, fair skin and a mischievous grin. We considered

Aunty Glad a cockney as by the time I was around she had long moved away and lived in Borehamwood, Hertfordshire. This was scarcely pie and eel territory but her Leafield accent had been layered with the sound of London suburbs and was quite different from the rest of the family.

Mum's next sister Daisy figured much more in my childhood. She was tall with a long face and jaw and an easy tooth-and-gums laugh. She laughed a lot and visited us often at Kingston Road. This was good news for me as she usually slipped me a shilling and it enabled me to gaze at the mystery of her missing little finger. She would hold her hand up to display its absence as if it wore a diamond ring. I think it was lost in a work accident. She often came into Oxford from Eynsham where she lived with her husband Victor Quainton. I have a sense that she had either just been to or was about to go to the Clarendon Hotel in Cornmarket in the centre of Oxford. This was a great meeting place for the American and other servicemen stationed near the city. Daisy liked what would have then been called a good time. Possibly a very good time. One of her brothers-in-law cruelly said of her, "She'd cock her arse at any besom."

She and Vic had no children. I know now that as a young woman Daisy had become pregnant by an older man referred to as "a jockey", probably a groom at a local farm. She had swallowed, or been given, something to abort the foetus and had been poisoned. She was taken to Burford Hospital. My grandfather, so the story went, bicycled over from Leafield to see her and on the way back stopped to clamber over a stone wall into a field to pray for her. The hospital could not do much to help and Daisy was sent home in effect to die. Fred insisted she get plenty of fresh air and moved her bed outside in the daytime. Eventually, she recovered. This may well account for the absence of children.

We often went to see Daisy and Victor in their little cottage in Acre End Street, Eynsham. I liked Vic. He had a deep, gravelly Oxfordshire voice and told stories of unlikely local characters, of the strange rituals of the Oddfellows glimpsed through the window of The Swan pub, of men falling drunk into the ditch and confusing a policeman with an angel of the Lord. Victor worked as a compositor at the Alden Press, a hundred-year-old printing firm in West Oxford. He gave me proof copies of books, among them the Swallows and Amazons series. Mind you, I couldn't get on with those awful precious children with the silly names.

When we went for tea - it was in their house that memorably I first ate a pickled onion with a cold beef sandwich - Victor would sit and tell stories while Daisy busied herself with the food. She was often aided in this by a short, dapper and very polite Polish chap, an airman, I learned, who could not return to Communist Poland or he would be "skinned alive". He was evidently very much at home. His position in the house was never clear to me as a small boy. Uncle Vic appeared unperturbed by his presence. Had I been a little older or quicker on the uptake my parents name for him, "The Polish Warrior", might have signalled why Aunty Daisy liked having him around. Or just having him, I guess.

A visit to Eynsham would conclude with the grown-ups going for a drink usually at The Star or The Evenlode, while David and I sat outside with Smiths crisps and lemonade. It was only a few miles into Oxford from there on the A40 but the road crosses the River Evenlode and runs close to the Thames. Fog rose from the low-lying fields and the little Morris 8 would fill with anxiety as Dad gripped the wheel, leaning forward to peer into the grey blanket ahead.

If the Wyatt women were chatterboxes, the Hooper men were taciturn, conversing at times only in grunts. Uncle Walter, Mum's only older brother, was a man of few words but powerful presence. He was tall, with a large strong head, a nose rather like Mum's and greying fair hair swept back Tarzan like. I could tell that he had always been protective of Mum and she looked up to him. She told David and me stories of his youth. He was thought by the village to be lonesome, lost in his own thoughts but a hard worker and determined. He played cricket and when the village played Chadlington each player took the name of a famous cricketer. Walter's view of himself is seen in his choice of P.G.H. Fender, a dashing all-rounder who in 1920 had scored a hundred in 35 minutes, a record that stood for more than sixty years. Walter claimed to be the fastest bricklayer in Oxfordshire. A figure of a thousand in an hour was mentioned, but that would have been fastest in the world.

Walter began building houses for sale in the thirties, among them the house Mum and Dad owned on the Eynsham Road and the house for his parents in Leafield. He founded Hooper and Jones Ltd. with a partner and developed many houses around Oxford, including those in Evelyn Close off the Botley Road, named after my mother's middle name. He always employed his brother Stanley as a bricklayer and Johnny as a labourer. Walter also operated as a bookie and at the end of the Second World War hit trouble. A 50-1 outsider called Airborne won the 1946 Derby. The Oxford and Bucks Light Infantry had been part of the Sixth Airborne Division and many local bets had been laid on this outsider. Stanley collected bets for Walter and assuming these bets were no hopers decided to stand the risk them himself. Either Walter or Stanley or both could not meet the liabilities. I was never sure how they emerged from this. Gambling debts were not enforceable in law so perhaps they just reneged on all the wives' two bob each-ways; perhaps they paid out over time.

Walter's building business went from strength to strength. He acquired a large Jaguar followed by a Rolls Royce and racehorses. He had married Aggie, five years older, when he was only twenty. She was a lovely person and they had two children. Sometime in my childhood the marriage ended and Walter set up home with a new family along the road from where we were later to live.

Mum's brother, Reg, another bricklayer, lived in Clapham with his wife Ivy. Reg said little and looked at you with a shy grin as if you were about to catch him out, should he chance to speak. We went to visit them once. Their London terrace house was dark and gloomy but it contained a wonder, an acre of green baize on what I took to be a full size (but was probably half size) snooker table. The males played. I felt inducted into mysteries of grown-upness as we moved quietly round the table, examining angles with a frown, as if a mistake might lead to loss of life. This triggered a family liking for snooker and, when we moved, a quarter size model that could sit on the dining room table arrived one Christmas. When Ivy died, Reg moved back to live in Leafield and built himself a house next door to the family home. It was he who made the concrete model of the village church. He had an occasionally acrimonious relationship with his neighbours, the two brothers who had never left, Stan and John.

Stan had the large heavy face of his father and the fair complexion of his mother. He was another brickie and he and John worked for Walter's firm. Stan had shiny cheeks and a mischievous grin but was frugal with words. He liked to poach, he liked to go to the races, he liked to hide his money. He was iffy about banks and when paying for expensive items, would startle shop assistants by turning away, furtively reaching for his wad and turning back with a handful of notes. It was always claimed in the family that he kept his money under the floorboards. Many years later my cousin Anne went to help clean up the Leafield house and found the actual hiding place. She opened a bedroom cupboard to discover, hanging from a rail, the bottom half of a pair of pyjamas, the legs sown up and the garment stuffed full of ten, twenty and fifty pound notes. Stan had limited outgoings and did not like to spend but had one extravagance, a good car. In the sixties, the two brothers set off for the Newbury dealers where they were to purchase a new Jaguar with Johnny in the passenger seat, a hold hall of cash between his legs and a loaded shotgun cradled in his arms. It was Stan's way.

Johnny was what the village In those days would have called "a bit simple" or a bit "Harry and Willy". He was bald with ruddy cheeks, his whole head like a rosy apple. When he spoke, it was with a strong Leafield accent in a high-pitched voice. He was called "Squeaker" at work. After a drink or two would sing in a pleasing tenor, his favourite being "I'll take you home again, Kathleeeeen". At a family party he once came into the room to sing dressed in a duffle coat and top hat. "Who are you meant to be?" asked someone. "Fisherman," he replied. His chief mode of communication with children and women was a huge and oft repeated wink accompanied by a sideways nod and a childlike grin. When questioned by the police about a poaching episode he adopted the strategy he used in answer to most questions.

"What were you doing there?"

Indicating Stan, he replied, "Ask 'im."

"Why did you have the gun with you?"

"Ask 'im."

It was the same if you asked if he was going to Newbury races, "Ask 'im." And he would give a little wobble of his head rather as many Indians do. I don't think that he could read or write well. When picking a horse to back in a race he would plump for an easily recognisable name. I remember him pointing out "Oxo" and "Danny B".

Johnny was so guileless he was hard not to like. As a boy I think I assumed that there was something wrong with him. Adults behaved as they might towards a child. He was teased, of course, as such people are and would become suddenly angry, shouting, "Shut your bloody row, Hewett," to one of his brothers-in-law. When petrol was still rationed he and Stan left our house in Kingston Road late one Christmas to discover that the petrol in their car had been siphoned off. Johnny, outraged, spoke at length, "One o'clock, bloody midnight and somebody's been an' milked 'er".

My favourite relation and Mum's closest sibling was Phyllis. She was the person above all with whom Mum enjoyed "a bit of old buck". (That was good "old buck", a chat. Not to be confused with bad "old buck", answering back or arguing, which is what I did prompting the rebuke, "Don't you give me any of that old buck.") Aunty Phyl was a few years younger than Mum with a pretty, cheeky face and always ready for "a bit of fun". She was married to Ronald Hewett, an ex-policeman who had been commissioned as a captain in the occupying forces in France at the end of the war. He had been invalided out after a jeep crash which left him with a deep, impressive scar on his forehead. This hinted at war hero to me, while Dad, no doubt a bit envious, made a point of referring to Ron as "Captain Hewett", thinking that he made too much of the stint in the army. Ron had a rich voice with a slight Oxfordshire accent and an air of authority. He had started a successful electrical business in Newbury. He was a teetotaller; Aunty Phyl liked a drink. They had a daughter, my cousin Anne, whom I looked up to, not least because I thought she looked like Doris Day, and she could sing, too. They played a regular part of our family year. When I was small, Ron, who would have liked a son, spent many days before Christmas making me a fort for my toy soldiers and a garage for toy cars.

This maternal family that I knew as a child was not quite the family that Mum grew up with, as I discovered in my forties. For a start, lovely, cuddly Aunty Glad had been very cuddly indeed. She had three children out of wedlock by three different fathers. The first of these, conceived when Glad was seventeen and a maid in a grand house in London, was Phyllis. So, Mum's favourite sister was her niece, my favourite aunt was my cousin, my favourite cousin was my cousin once removed. When my inquiries into the family history revealed this there were ructions and tears of shame and anger from Mum and Phyl. They had carried this all too common secret with them into the respectable world of their adult lives. Now I had burgled their secrets. It did calm down. Gladys' second child was uncle, now cousin, Reg, conceived and born in Leafield. The third was Big John, who had been born in London and lived with Gladys and her husband in Borehamwood.

Then there was simple Johnny, again not my uncle but another cousin, the child of Mum's sister Bertha. There were even stories in the village that he was the offspring of Bertha and her father. I think this was just gossip, inspired by the notion that Johnny, "not all there" as they would have said, was what one might imagine an inbred boy to be like. So, my uncles, the unmarried brothers Stan and John were not brothers but brother and nephew and, what is more, Stan had been married and fathered a child.

Someone else never mentioned was another of Annie's daughters, Mary Jane, known as Ginny. She became a nurse in London and married in Marylebone. There may have been a child. By the Second World War she was a patient in Littlemore Hospital, the Oxford "loony bin", as I would have known it. She lived until 1984 and was in some sort of sheltered accommodation very close to us. My parents used to visit her but never a word to David or me. When I learned all this, I put it to Mum. "Yes," she said, "Ginny was a nurse. She went funny." That was that.

So, by the end of the First World War, the saintly Annie Hooper had been bringing up three grandchildren as her own. And while she served as an admired model for my mother, the family in general definitely did not. Four illegitimate children, something shameful if common then, three brought up as my mother's siblings; an early divorce with an unseen child and a sister with mental illness, a further flag of shame in the forties and fifties. I suppose Mum simply wanted all this hidden and forgotten. Where would you begin to tell a seven-year-old, she might have thought? But a seven-year-old takes the world as he finds it. What is, just is. It would have been no odder than wondering why Johnny conversed mainly in winks, why "'Ow do?" was the greeting for strangers and "'Ow bist gwain arn?" the greeting for family.

Leafield school was on the village green where it is today. Mum kept her exercise books and as a boy I was impressed by her careful drawings and the neatness of the writing and layout. She enjoyed school but the leaving age was fourteen, she had to work and work meant going into service like her elder sisters Glad and Daisy. The latter never settled into it and had set off several times for positions as a maid only to chuck it in after a day or so, returning home even before her trunk of luggage had arrived at her placement. Mum now left for a position as maid ten miles away in Bampton. "I hated it, shut up and hidden away. It was like a prison." She next worked at a house in Witney where after only a month she was accused of stealing. Telling me about it sixty years later, the very thought of the accusation brought tears. "My mother was honest, very correct, a lady." Her mother came to take her away. It transpired that one of the sons of the house was the culprit.

Mum had only good things to say about her next employer, a first link to the university. Mrs Heaton and her husband, Dr Trevor Heaton, a don at Christ Church, lived in the centre of Oxford at 37 St Giles, a handsome late Georgian stone house owned by the college. The Heatons, Mum told us, "were wonderful people, strict but kind." Mum's domestic standards were much influenced by her time with Mrs Heaton, as she instructed us, "Sit up straight!" "Don't put your elbows on the table!" "Don't slouch!" "Never eat in the street!" "Pull your chair up!" "Don't talk with your mouth full!" "Don't hold your knife and fork like a pencil!" The Heatons addressed Mum by her first name, Hettie. She was a house maid whose jobs included lighting the fires and cleaning. She made a lifelong friend there in Anne, the parlour maid, who married a farmer, the source of our extra victuals during rationing.

A favourite story was how when she was in still in her teens at Mrs Heaton's, Mum was allowed home on Boxing Day. She took the train from Oxford to Ascott-under-Wychwood station, from where it was a three-mile walk to Leafield. She set off in the snow, which began falling ever more thickly and drifting. The going became hard and she was eventually forced to a halt, knocking on the door of a farm cottage where she thought she knew the inhabitants. The people had moved and a poor family was now living there. They took her in and Mum, whose family knew hard times, was shocked by their condition. "They had nothing," she told us. Mum had to stay overnight and was able to reach home the following day. When Mrs Heaton heard the story after the holiday, she helped the family.

When Mum left 37 St Giles to become a waitress at the Cadena Café, Mrs Heaton came to see her after work to check how she was. Mum hated it there and was offered a job as maid to the wife of the principal of Jesus College. She named Mrs Heaton as a reference and her former employer immediately warned her off: the people were impossibly strict and locked out staff if not in by ten. The stories Mum told of her life in domestic service, with the happy exception of the Heatons, conjured a grim picture of middle-class employers. The next, Miss Malham, from a family of Oxford solicitors, only allowed Mum out on her afternoon off if she took the dog for a walk. Was this an Oxford thing, professionals and academics demonstrating their status? Was it the same everywhere, the middle class barely affording what they felt entitled to? Was it just thoughtlessness? Whatever the reasons, these stories filled the grow bag that nourished my early politics.

In 1928 the Heatons bought Garsington Manor from Philip and Lady Ottoline Morrell and moved in. Soon their maid was in the family way. Mrs Heaton did not wish to sack the girl, who coincidently had relations in Leafield, but needed someone for six months while she went off to have her baby. She asked Mum who didn't think she would like being out in the country after living in Oxford but went. Mum was mortified when the girl returned to work and "told Mrs Heaton all about my family, about Bertha and that. After I had gone to help out." The "that" no doubt referred to her family's collection of illegitimate offspring. The girl was probably trying to recapture some pride by revealing that the Hoopers also had their hidden shame, and in quadruplicate. For Mum the hurt remained. Above all, she was protective of the honour of her mother, Annie Hooper. "Mrs Heaton thought a lot of my mother. Some of the others' mothers were rough country women. But my mother was a lady."

She remained in touch with Mrs Heaton for more than thirty years, occasionally asking advice. After her time at Garsington, Hettie found a job in the middle of Oxford at Twining's Wine Lounge on the second floor of a building on the corner of Cornmarket and Market Street. She liked being in town, she liked the superior pretensions of the business and she liked the clientele, which included undergraduates and journalists from the *Oxford Mail* and *Times*. The other assistant was a Miss Goldhawk, who, according to Mum liked the drink too much.

"She used to get off with the undergrads and take them upstairs, she did."

"What was upstairs?" the boy Wyatt asked.

"Rooms," she replied.

This would not have been Hettie's way in any circumstances. What is more, she was now going strong with Basil. He was working for a firm that won a contract to build a monastery in Yorkshire and asked if he would go to work on it. He liked the idea, it would be good experience. Hettie thought otherwise, "If you go that will be the finish with us." He remained and they became engaged.

There were bumps in the road. One evening Hettie was returning from the wine lounge to her lodging when she saw her husband-to-be coming out of a pub at closing time. As it happened, he had been at home all evening and just popped over for a late pint but Hettie assumed otherwise. He received a letter saying that she did not want to be married to a man who was always at the pub, enclosing a pound note, the first he had given her to save up. His mother caught sight of it and asked,

"What's up, Bas? Had a row with Hettie?" He put it back in the envelope and replied,

"Oh no. She just wants me to get her something."

That evening he hurried to the wine lounge to explain and they patched up the quarrel. Thereafter, he went to Twinings a couple of nights a week, drank orange squash as it sold no beer - only wine and cocktails - and walked Hettie home.

They saved. Basil worked some evenings and weekends for Hettie's brother, Walter, who was just beginning to buy land and build houses for sale. He started on some three bedroom semi-detached houses on the Eynsham Road and the engaged couple asked him to keep one for them, one of the last to be completed as they wanted maximum time to save up. The wedding was planned for 14 September 1935 in Leafield. The house cost £400 and they had a mortgage for £450 leaving £50 to buy furniture. They went to the Port of London Cabinet Works for a front room suite, a sideboard and bedroom furniture, to Maples in Bournemouth for a front room carpet and bought some second-hand pieces from Basil's sister. Dad used to tell me that the biggest thrill of his life was the morning of the wedding when sister-in-law to be Phyllis and her husband Ronald, who were to drive him to Leafield, took him to look at 135 Eynsham Road. Few working people owned their house in those days and here was his and Hettie's, all ready to move into with two easy chairs waiting either side of the fireplace.

The reception was in Leafield village hall. Dad's eldest brother, Bill, gave a speech which like most wedding speeches was too long. Their honeymoon was an evening at the New Theatre in Oxford with Phyl and Ron to see *The Chocolate Soldier*, a popular operetta by Oscar Straus. For the rest of her life Aunty Phyl teased them that when she and Ron dropped them off at their new house after the show on their wedding night, they had asked, "Won't you come in?" They were both 28 years old. Strange as it may seem, as a boy I wondered why they married so late in life. Twenty-eight seemed ancient when all around us in the fifties people were marrying at twenty-one. I wasn't born until they had been married more than six years when Mum was nearly 35, David when she was forty. They were a prudent couple determined to take on only what they could afford. This was a time of delayed gratification.

Kingston Road 1950. Our house the second shop front from left. Police box on corner the target for pea-shooting.

6
DOWN PORT MEADOW

One of my earliest memories is the sound of the wooden wheels of Dad's handcart crunching grit as he pushed it on the road. The cart was a wooden platform with low sides which rode on two spoked wagon wheels and was pushed with two shafts that also helped balance it. A leg on each shaft was well off the ground when in motion but provided support when stationary. With this Dad transported tins of paint, ladders, tools and timber, which he kept in the big shed at the bottom of our garden.

He was now working for himself. When Organs had been directed to work on bomb damage in and around London, Dad went with them. In time, Mum who was coping with the infant me and running the wine shop and who was always prone to anxiety, had become depressed. When it was a weekend for Dad to stay in London she made him a cake which Mr Organ would take when he visited his men. One week she asked him to tell Dad that she was not well and needed him in Oxford for a bit. Old man Organ took the cake but not the message so when Dad was next home he found his wife upset that he had not responded. He could not just leave Organs as wartime labour controls directed who worked where, so he went with Hettie to the doctor and obtained a letter saying that she needed looking after. With this he secured the authority to remain in Oxford and care for her. He tried to get her into company as much as possible, often with a drink at The Gardener's Arms in Plantation Road. I think she must have been quite seriously unwell for Dad told me that there were times in my childhood when he thought she might never throw off her depression.

My parents were living on their savings and Mum's modest earnings from the shop. This could not go on indefinitely. Dad went to his brother-in-law, Walter, who gave him a house painting job. With a jam jar and two new paint brushes he set to work. This was his first step on his own. He found other painting jobs in Kingston Road as people had not been able to get simple maintenance work done during the war. He worked for local builders. His brother, Ron, introduced him to Eagleston and Son, ironmongers who sold fireplaces which Dad then installed, 200 of them in Jesus College. He put a sign above the front door at 15 Kingston Road, "Painter and Decorator and General Repairs". He bought the handcart, ladders and some scaffolding. He found a labourer, Ernie Bowerman, to work with him.

He told me how one day he was pushing his handcart past a building site in North Oxford where elder brother Frank was in charge. The foreman on a big site was the company sergeant-major of the building trade. Frank was one, Basil had been one. Now, Frank called his men to laugh at the sight of his brother reduced to a jobbing private. Basil didn't mind. He was his own man, was doing well, Hettie was getting better and he had a son.

I think he always had plenty of work. He was a careful, conscientious craftsman who won many returning clients over the years. He would trundle off up Leckford Road to a job in Parktown or along Kingston Road to paint a house in Farndon Road. Before long he bought a small army surplus Austin covered van. The open platform was protected with khaki canvas thrown over three metal hoops. A back flap came down for loading supported by two canvas-sheathed chains. This enabled him to travel to more distant sites. and provided hours of happy clambering in and out for me and friends when it was parked in Longworth Road. He took no test and before long was stopped for something by the police. He admitted that he had no driving licence but avoided prosecution because it transpired that his 1930s motor cycle licence qualified him to drive a car or van and was still valid in the late forties.

He could now bid for and win larger contract work. Some of this was private but the great majority was council building. One and a half million homes were built in the ten years after 1945. In Oxfordshire Dad built council houses and bungalows. The sound track of my childhood rang with names of the villages where he worked: Curbridge (the first), Stanton Harcourt, Long Hanborough, Souldern, Bladon, Great Haseley, Stanton St John, Old Marston and more. He added bathrooms to houses in Wolvercote and extensions to the schools in Bladon and Woodstock. He built police houses in Headington and on the new Blackbird Leys estate.

Alongside the litany of villages were the names of men who worked for or with Dad, "Old Backabit", "Tripey" Howes, "Goldfly" Coppock and others. If a workman or supplier didn't come up to scratch, then "He didn't know whether his arse was bored or punched". Dad was averse to show offs who would "bum the chat", checking something out he would "give it the once over", if he wanted some room he'd say, "Let the dog see the rabbit," and appealing for fairness, "Play the white man, darkie." This last picked up when he was a young man. Dad placed great store by fairness both in the world at large and between his sons.

I loved it when he took me to one of his sites, stepping over foundations where walls would soon rise, peering into plastered but unpainted rooms, looking up to the wooden skeleton of the roof to be. On the ground were piles of bricks awaiting their turn, hundredweight paper bags of cement bursting to release their flowery contents, bright sand mountains often signed with dog crap, irregular grey scars where mortar had been mixed. I loved, and still do, the smell of newly sawn timber and fresh paint. I liked the musical swish swash of the broad distemper brushes at their employ, the imposing clang of a dropped scaffolding pole, the neat snap as Dad closed his folding ruler.

For all this, for all that I loved and admired my father, I'm not sure why but I don't think that I ever aspired to be bricklayer. Mind you, I did see it as proper man's work, unlike tall, skinny Mr Butler's.

He wore a collar and tie to work. I remember watching his strange prancing walk as he passed our house on his way to the University Press and thinking that I could never do a job that a woman could do.

After a meal when he arrived home, Dad would most evenings do what he called "the booking", which, unlike bricklaying, he didn't much enjoy. This was not just keeping track of expenditure and hours worked but estimating for new contracts. He employed someone to help him with this, Ted Skuse, a smiling presence one evening a week. Ted was tall and had been in the Life Guards, of which he was justly proud. I liked him but thought it a great joke, as did my parents, to pretend to forget how tall he was and ask him week after week. "Six feet two and a half," was the reply. He never forgot the half.

It was only after the booking that Dad would enjoy a bottle of beer. Mum liked what she called "a drop of old crater", a whisky. In later years both would always take a hot toddy, whisky, sugar and hot water, up to bed with them. Dad liked a beer with Sunday lunch. In spite of the G. T. Jones shop, they never had wine in the house in Kingston Road. Much later when it did occasionally appear it was Sauternes, of which Mum spoke with some reverence.

She must have given up the shop in the late forties after David was born. She now had two sons to bring up. Her mental handbook for this task she compiled from the lessons her mother had taught her and what she had learned in service. She placed huge emphasis on knowing right from wrong. I'm not sure that the name of Jesus was much or ever mentioned in this regard. Doing the right thing was just what you did. While she was happy to have black market food from her farmer's wife friend Auntie Anne, she would not have the tea Dad bought at the army base he worked on early in the war. It was a supply depot for distributing food to army and RAF camps.

Naturally, as soon as the food began to arrive a black market sprang up, the building workers paying a sergeant for the scarce food. Dad had his lunch tin filled with tea in return for a packet of cigarettes. He took it proudly home to show Hettie. She refused to accept it. The Annie Hooper in her spoke, "It wasn't his to give, take it back." Dad could hardly do that so he hid it in a drawer and secretly slipped a little into their tea caddy each week until it was used up.

Dad was miffed. The other men were having sugar, butter, bacon and joints of meat from the depot and his wife would let him have none of it. He earthed his resentment by spreading the word one Friday that the departing lorry was to be searched by military police. For a while at least his colleagues were afraid to make their trades.

I didn't shoplift even so much as a sweet cigarette or a packet of Spangles as a child and never have. This grounding has stayed with me. If I am undercharged in a shop or restaurant I have to tell them. I have never and could never strike a woman. I am not boasting of moral choices here. I have made no choices: somehow Mum made them for me. How did this square with letting me tiptoe back to school to retouch the eleven plus papers? It must have been Mr Gray's ploy. He was a head teacher, a person of some standing. If he suggested it, then why not? If there was a black market and he was farming exam results, accept the offer. I wonder if my parents hesitated to go along with it. Somehow, I doubt it.

Other chapters in Mum's handbook were aspirational. She sought to display and for us to learn proper behaviour, whether this was saying, "Hello" politely or eating bread and butter with fish and chips (one of her employers must have done this). Her eyes were ever cast upwards. There was no greater compliment on someone's manners and behaviour than "very refined". The greatest accolade was "proper gentry". They were in the best possible way well above our class. While we could never be gentry, we could make a good impression. It was implicit that one should try to gain acceptance. I think this influenced me in both behaviour and ambition. I wasn't one, but could I pass for one?

How important, then, it was for me to follow her mother's rubric and take care to catch my "golden ball". Mum impressed upon me that it would only fall once; the chance must be taken. She identified this moment as getting into Magdalen College School and needing to make the most of it. Yet it arrived again when I took my O Level exams, also when A Levels loomed and she proclaimed it equally confidently when I sat the Cambridge entrance exam. She was right. It might have rained golden balls, but drop one of them and there may be no more.

Mum had her own Leafield argot. If she didn't know where something was or didn't want to tell you ("Where have you put my savings certificates, Mum?") it was "up in Annie's room behind the clock." If it looked cloudy in the distance, "It's looking rough over Will's mum's." To an arch comment about a family member's behaviour she would add, "Not mentioning any names but where my eyes goes." If someone lost their temper, he was "in a twaiging".

My parents did row at times and I remember interposing myself between them so they would stop. And we did get smacked or very occasionally worse. Someone Dad had worked for had given him a horn handled riding crop, not that anyone in the family ever had nor ever would ride. The only part horses played in the Wyatts' life was on the racecourse. The crop was kept in a clothes cupboard and twice when I must have been even naughtier than usual (probably being horrid to Mum) he fetched it and struck me hard on the thigh with it. The second time it left two red weals. I could tell afterwards that he was not just sorry but ashamed at what he had done. He was in fact a very gentle man. This was quite out of character. Thereafter the crop remained in the cupboard save for when it enabled me to urge home a fantasy Derby winner.

I must have been aware that a warm and happy home was not the lot of all children. I know that I felt an instinctive sorrow for some of the boys with black plimsolls, boys who looked pale or spindly, boys who carried an anxious expression, the wary, threatened look only an adult's face should carry. In my complacency, I guess I was sorry for any boys who didn't have my Mum and Dad as parents. I occupied a warm, safe and protected place in the world. I knew that bad things would not happen to David and me. I looked out with the benevolent gaze of a fresh faced, fair haired boy Pollyanna.

The family went to church at Christmas and Easter and I was enrolled at Sunday School. This took place at nine o'clock on Sunday morning at the rear of Phil and Jim church. We sat on little wooden chairs and listened to Bible stories. The chief attraction was my attendance book for which we were given a coloured stamp of a scene from the life of Jesus each time we turned up. I picked up the unsettling notion that God was in our heads, listening to all our thoughts so I should be "good". If I did dwell on this, it was only ever momentarily. I said my prayers each evening before bed. They were brief, the important bit being the end, "God bless David and God bless Mummy and Daddy." It seemed to work.

The 29th Oxford wolf cub pack I joined at seven was attached to St Margaret's Church, and held its meetings in the church hall in Polstead Road, a quarter of a mile further down Kingston Road from our house. This brought a first uniform, important for a lad just four years after the end of the war. The green jumper and khaki shorts were the base, the best of it being the yellow neckerchief with red edging which was folded to provide a small triangle at the rear and threaded through the woggle at the front into two carefully matching twists.

First test, "Know the composition of the Union Flag and the right way to fly it; know in simple form the stories of the Saints of England, Scotland and Ireland." I accumulated enough badges to indicate that the skill level required was pretty humble: knots - "reef and sheet bend" then "clove hitch and bowline", somersault, leap frog, hopping, ball, balance exercises - "Walk upright and with a good carriage carrying a solid article weighing about two pounds on his head, without using his hands, for a distance of about ten yards, turn and come back to the starting point", nature study, tidiness, highway code, compass and "Understand the meaning of thrift in all things and be carrying it out in practice." Not sure how I passed that one.

To my surprise, for I have just checked, these tests though so redolent of that post war era still obtain. I wore the badges proudly on my sleeves along with, in time, a single tape band for the office of "seconder" and a double band for "sixer". The pack was presided over by our amiable Akela, a stocky chap probably in his thirties, also in shorts. He invited one or two of us, and we were allowed by parents to accept the invitation, to his house for a couple of hours of board games, biscuits and lemonade. He must have been lonely or attracted to boys or a bit emotionally stunted or generally nerdy, or probably all of these. He had to deal firmly with Jeremy Taylor and me when a brownie envoy came with a message from her pack and the two of us lay down on the floor trying to see her knickers (again!). We were sent home for letting down the 29th. We didn't go home as we would have had to explain why we had been expelled. The pack went out tracking that evening and Jeremy and I hung around trying to ingratiate ourselves by pretending we might be helpful if someone got lost. We were re-admitted the following week.

At eleven I moved to the 42nd Oxford Sea Scouts. This was a Phil and Jim troop and met in the church hall in which the school lunches were served. I left after a couple of years as we moved and homework began to take its toll. A note tells me that I earned eight pounds seven shillings in Bob a Job week. This was when scouts knocked on doors and offered to do a job for a bob, a shilling (five pence today), raising funds for the scout movement. Tasks varied from running an errand to sweeping the front steps, cleaning a bicycle to hoovering a room. Often the householder would reward you with two shillings or half a crown but not always. I remember a long, hot hour or more pushing a grass mower for just one measly bob.

I think the Sea Scouts had a boat on the river at Medley on Port Meadow but I never went in it. Port Meadow was in any case the chief landscape of my outdoor play. It comprises more than 400 acres of common land between the Oxford to Worcester railway line and the River Thames. Apart from a few archaeological bumps it is flat and often flooded. It is said to have been given to the freemen of Oxford by Alfred the Great, has never been ploughed and the freemen of the city still have the right to graze their animals on it and do so. In the holidays, some afternoons after school or Saturday mornings friends and I walked a hundred yards down Longworth Road from the end of the alley behind our garden to the junction with Southmoor Road and into Walton Well Road. There was a handsome Victorian drinking fountain on the corner but I never knew anyone make use of it. On the left was Lucy's, the Eagle Iron works. It had made munitions during the war and now electrical engineering products as well as iron castings. Jeremy Taylor's uncle worked there and brought him offcuts of a hard plastic-like material that Jeremy showed off to us in a conspiratorial way: "That's special stuff, that is, called Bakelite." His uncle was in a "secret organisation" called Toc H, he said. We were suitably impressed by its code-like name. (It was a Christian-based charity originally of servicemen's clubs in the First World War.)

The road to the meadow continued over the Oxford Canal via bridge 242. Many times we would descend to the towpath here to go fishing. The water was the colour of fresh cow poo but we caught silvery dace, whiskery gudgeon, red-tinged roach and chub. In summer, carrying a Swiss roll of towel and swimming costume under the arm, we walked half a mile along the canal towpath over railway and river on a footbridge to swim at Tumbling Bay. Two pools, deep and shallow, had been created between weirs on a backwater of the Thames. You undressed in the very basic wooden changing place, swam and messed about for an hour or two and trod home tired with towel round your neck and wet cozzy on a stick over your shoulder, the delicious smell of the river on your skin.

If not down to the canal, we continued to the red and blue-grey brick bridge over Castle Mill Stream and the next over the railway. The middle section, above the rails, was of metal sheets with a flat riveted metal parapet a couple of feet wide. I saw tougher, braver boys, probably from Barney school, walk along this thirty feet above the tracks. At the far end where the brick bridge ended there was a gap on the left you could climb through to slide down the smooth top of the curved brick buttress. It was twenty feet or more down to a precious patch of ground by a narrow rivulet that ran alongside the railway. We would lie flat on our stomachs and descend feet first, steering with our insteps. When Christopher Honey first tried it we watched helpless as he allowed his feet to dangle over the edge and thus fall with a shout and a thump to the ground. His legs were not hurt but his face scraped the bricks as he fell, cutting his chin from one side to the other. Blood poured from the wound and I led him crying and bleeding back up to his house, across the street from ours. His chin needed half a dozen or more stitches.

The little stream by the bridge was bordered with reeds. We picked the stronger looking specimens and pressed them between our fingers to accentuate the V shape of the sharp-edged leaves. To our eyes, they made convincing skiffs to which we could carefully add tiny pebbles as the crew to create entries for Oxford versus Cambridge boat races. In the water they soon tipped over or became stuck but we minded little. The preparation was all. The Oxford-Cambridge boat race was a major annual event in the consciousness of a small Oxford boy. It was the chief manifestation of the little understood university as far as I was concerned.

Nearby a concrete bridge led to a gate giving onto the railway tracks. This was the chosen pitch for trainspotting. You could walk onto the rails to see if trains were approaching, place pennies on the line to have them satisfyingly pressed smooth and shiny and, above all, identify the passing steam engines. They hauled passenger trains of the brown and cream livery of the Great Western Railway or goods trains of wooden sided wagons. We each had the Ian Allen GWR trainspotting book, lists of the engine numbers by their different classes, from the humble square-tanked shunters with numbers but no names, through the grander named Hall, Manor, Castle and County classes up to the highly prized, but rarely seen in Oxford, King class. When you saw an engine number you "copped" it, underlining it in the book with pen and ruler. There was much boasting and one-upmanship about copping, say, Denbigh Castle or County of Hereford, rather than the smaller, humble workhorse tankers. It was very much a boy thing, just a form of collecting and tabulating. The engines were the attraction: the speed, the coal smell, the hissing and panting as they passed. Some boys travelled to Didcot for the day to spot engines on the Wales and West Country trains. The gate by the allotments on the Hereford and Worcester line sufficed for me.

If we were fishing in the river, we would take the bushy path we called Willow Walk which followed an arc of the slow, sulky Castle Mill Stream to where it met the Thames by the bailey bridge. Pollarded willows shielded the meadow side, hawthorn and the white bonbons of snowberries decorated the water side. We mostly fished just a short way along with bread our usual bait. There was much lore and discussion about the optimum size of hook, purchased in small transparent packets, and style of float, long thin quill or short stubby cork. The float was held vertical with split lead shot weights which we bit to attach to the line. We threw back any fish we caught after the sometimes simple, sometimes messy business of holding the soapy scales and disgorging the hook. I returned home with the thick fishy smell on my fingers, the sweet smell of success. When we ventured further to fish in the Thames proper I thought it very advanced to try ledgering, bottom fishing with a single lead weight, but it was never a success.

The main way to the meadow itself was through a cattle gate at the bottom of Walton Well Road. Through that to the right was a large expanse of allotments, to the left rough grass, studded with crusty cow pats and thistles in summer, which was our football and cricket ground. Ahead a path led through the summer ragwort to the bailey bridge. I was five when the Royal Engineers erected the prefabricated bridge in an afternoon to replace a wooden bridge swept away in floods. I remember the excitement when my parents took me down to see it, most likely on that first day, as we met neighbours in the crowd that gathered. The flat bridge crosses the Thames to the thin Fiddler's Island strung with cabin cruiser moorings. This sliver of land separates the navigable and unnavigable branches of the river. At its north end, the nineteenth-century Rainbow Bridge arches its iron latticework across the main branch to the west bank near a small boatyard. This was another good fishing spot. Some big boys occasionally jumped from the top of the bridge.

A little way along the meadow side of the river were tiny beaches, known as Sandy Bay. Families used to picnic on the grass here and go swimming. I have a dim memory of water and shouting at one such Saturday afternoon picnic when I was three. My parents had to tell me what happened. Dad had gone in for a swim and was in the middle of the stream when I left off paddling in the shallows and began walking out into the current to join him. Did I disappear under or just nearly disappear? In any event, a neighbour who was with us saw what was happening and rushed in fully clothed to haul me out. In time it became rare to see anyone bathing there. Friends and I did so when we were in our teens and again got into trouble in a strong current, swimming to the opposite bank but having to turn back on the return and walk shamefacedly over two bridges to reach our clothes.

The nearest I ever came to stealing was on Port Meadow when Raymond Coates recruited one or two of us for a scrumping expedition in the allotments there. Our nerve failed. We wandered up and down between the plots, unable to pluck up the courage to lift anything from the neat rows of vegetables. What did we think we would we do with cabbages anyway? We bragged to each other about what we would take next time. One of the few people tending a plot that morning hailed us and, whether innocent of our nefarious aims or just taking pity on lads in a funk, offered us carrots. We accepted and slunk off behind a shed. Honour could only be gained by learning to smoke. Ray exuded a knowledgeable air and explained that he didn't have cigarettes but he did have string and he knew from his elder brother the effect was much the same. So, bits of string were cut with a penknife and we each put a piece in our mouth and lit the end. There was a little smoke to be sure. We looked encouragingly at each other in the certainty that this was big stuff. Three minutes of big stuff, anyway. I never did get around to smoking a cigarette.

Paraffin Annie was often seen on Port Meadow. I am sure that she was a sad soul, probably with mental illness. To us she was a mad, raggedy old lady pushing a little trolley around and talking to herself. We were a little bit afraid of her, a little amused. Neither my friends nor I teased her but some did. Just over Walton Well Bridge, in the scruffy area now a car park, a group of older boys used to hang around. We would observe them from afar as we made our way home from the meadow. They smoked, looked furtive and were often with an older man who limped. In some way we knew there were stories about this man and these boys, nothing specific but not good things. We knew we should steer clear. What were they up to? Was he a predatory homosexual? Was he just a man with a limp?

I never saw it myself but it was much reported and speculated upon by my friends: graffiti had appeared down by the meadow reading as follows, "any boy who would like to put his hands under a school girl's skirt and touch her quim meet me tonight." This sounded strangely inviting and yet mysterious, the quim being a hazily understood object of interest. Was it the same as Jeremy Taylor's sister's "little bum at the front"? It was surely something we weren't supposed to know about, let alone touch. Although that didn't sound an altogether bad idea. Who would make such an offer? Was it genuine? Did anyone try to take it up? For some reason, we assumed that it was made by a man. Was it the man with the limp? I had no mind to find out but the words lingered.

On the edge of the meadow, and more regularly along the canal, boys found little plastic sachets in the long grass. When they held them up to the light and squeezed them a viscous liquid moved within. They were called "johnnies". That we knew. What we could not fathom was what on earth they were for. It had to be something too forbidden and too grown up for us to know about. We struggled. Their most likely provenance was that they were something to do with the Yanks, the American servicemen we saw in the city. Yes, it had to be the Yanks. They had left them there. No-one knew why.

I was a goody-goody and did not join in needless to say, but I knew boys who definitely knew boys who went "prozzie watching". It was rumoured by those who knew these things that a prozzie lived just along the road from us, in the 170s of Kingston Road we thought. Prozzie watching entailed following the prozzies about. First you had to find your prozzie. The boys who did it apparently knew how. A much greater mystery to me was what a prozzie actually was. It was a woman, of course, any fool knew that, but what did they do that made them worth following? What might you see if you did? The way in which they were discussed suggested that they were well outside the life of the families we knew. They were probably bad, almost certainly rude. Men came into it somewhere. Money was mentioned, as well. By puzzling away, I came up with an answer. What with it being rude, the men involved, the house nearby, money, the secrecy - I had it. You went to visit a prozzie and you and other men gave her money, then you sat on the sofa in her front room (this is what you might be able to spy on perhaps). She would come into the room and take her blouse off so you could look at her tits. Probably so many shillings for five minutes and so many for ten. Ten whole minutes with her blouse off. Blimey!

The endless hours of childhood weren't filled only with fishing, playing on the meadow and wondering about rude stuff. On the rare occasions I made an entry in the pocket diary I received for Christmas it read, "Mucked about". This might have encompassed playing balloon football with David at the bottom of the stairs, playing marbles ("aggies") with friends on the pavement, practising spitting in that determined way men did in the street, playing with my toy soldiers (enemy always the Germans), playing cowboys, grinding ivy seeds between two earthenware tiles or using the election leaflet of the Conservative candidate, Lawrence Turner MP, as a darts target in Dad's shed. Mucking about was bobbing happily in a coracle on an infinite sea.

I wasn't much of a fighter but I threw one memorable punch. A big boy, Norris, came into the alley outside our back gate one day and started kicking my little brother David's toy car. I remonstrated so Norris turned on me. I told David to take his car and go into our garden then faced Norris and hit him as hard as I could on the nose. He could easily have thrashed me but was taken by surprise and I must have hurt him. Before he could gather himself, I turned and ran as fast as I could back through our gate and bolted it top and bottom. He shouted but the gate was too high to climb over. I was shaking. It was hardly a heroic battle but the plucky British had repelled the invader.

Sport began to occupy me, playing it, thinking about it, selecting perfect teams and so on. Oxford did not have a league side so I decided to support West Bromwich Albion. In 1949 two clubs were promoted from the second to the first division, Fulham and West Bromwich Albion. My dad claimed a fondness for Fulham going back to his time working on the bomb damage. Rather than like most sons who adopt their father's team, I declared in a bolshie move that I would follow Albion. The choice was quickly re-enforced as they had a successful side and paid a dividend in 1954, winning the FA Cup and coming close second in the league. Further confirmation that auspicious auguries had guided me came when we first went to see them play. The night before I dreamed that they won 7-1. A boy would, wouldn't he? On the day, they surpassed this and beat Manchester City by nine goals to two, their biggest win of the century. I remember seeing a Manchester City supporter crying in the stand as we left our seats.

A luxury for a sporty boy in Oxford was that the university cricket team played first class fixtures in the University Parks. The Parks was open to all so you could watch top county sides and some tourists free of charge. On May and June afternoons after school I often walked the half mile to see an hour or so of play. What was more, you could stand by the nets in the Easter holidays to watch the undergraduate players at practice as they competed for selection. The South Africans D.B. Hofmeyr and B. Boobyer were among their stars, and D.B. Carr, who played in both Pegasus Amateur Cup wins and was later Secretary of the Test and County Cricket board, was captain in 1950.

One late afternoon that year I was in the Parks, possibly or possibly not with friends, when I was approached by a man who asked the way to the Gents. I told him it was just on the other side of the pavilion but he asked if I would show him and I did. When we got there he ushered me inside and into a cubicle. He made me take my short trousers down and lean forward against the wall. I felt some sort of ointment rubbed on my bottom and then what I guessed was the tip of his cock in the same place. Very shortly after he, as I thought, peed on my bum. That was that. I pulled up my pants and shorts and continued the polite conversation we had begun on the way over. Did he say or did I put words in his mouth that this was all perfectly normal? Indeed, that he had to go about doing this to boys for some unspecified reason. The more I think about it the more I am sure that, in order to make everything as it should be, I created this important role for him. As we left he set off for the Keble College gate; my way home was via the Norham Gardens gate.

When I arrived home I told my mother about this interesting event. Her and Dad's reaction suggested that this had not been as routine an occurrence as I had presumed. A policeman arrived to ask me about what had happened. I think I may have been taken to the police station for examination. I do remember being asked about the man: how old was he? "About the same age as my Uncle Ron" was my reply. For some reason I knew that Ron was 38. Some days afterwards a policeman came to school and I was taken in his car to central Oxford, Queen Street, I think, where we sat in the stationary vehicle. I was asked to look at people in the street to see if I could spot the man. I didn't see him, and as far as I was concerned that was that. I never thought much about it again save when occasionally the urine and disinfectant smell of old Gents lavs reminded me.

I continued going to the Parks to watch cricket as the signatures in an old autograph book testify: D.B. Carr, F.S Trueman, N.W.D. Yardley, B. Statham, Cyril Washbrook, M.C. Cowdrey and more. In pairs we sometimes carried the cricket bags of visiting county players as they left the ground. The reward often sixpence. Not from Yorkshire's Len Hutton though. Mum and Dad, for all their concern, must have allowed this. Perhaps I was only allowed to go with a friend. The school did not forget the incident. On my end of the year report Mr Gray, the headmaster, wrote cryptically, "I am confident now that past history has not upset him. If he continues like this he will do well."

8

TO-DAY, AS ʌ
I send this per
all other boy:
you have sha
dangers of a
shared no le:
Allied Natioɪ

I know yoɩ
belong to a cc
of such supre
parents and ɩ
who by their
enterprise br
qualities be ᵥ
join in the cᵢ
among the n
and peace.

Letter from the King
Emperor to every
schoolchild.

7
WAR BABY

, 1946

EBRATE VICTORY,
message to you and
girls at school. For
the hardships and
war and you have
he triumph of the

lways feel proud to
which was capable
ort; proud, too, of
rothers and sisters
ge, endurance and
victory. May these
s you grow up and
effort to establish
of the world unity

George R.I.

still have my copy of the Second World War victory certificate sent to all schoolchildren. On one side a large coloured royal coat of arms dominates and beneath it is a letter from King George VI, dated 8 June 1946:

> To-day as we celebrate victory, I send this personal message to you and all other boys and girls at school. For you have shared in the hardships and dangers of a total war and you have shared no less in the triumph of the Allied Nations. I know you will always feel proud to belong to a country which was capable of such supreme effort; proud, too, of parents and elder brothers and sisters who by their courage, endurance and enterprise brought victory. May these qualities be yours as you grow up and join in the common effort to establish among the nations of the world unity and peace. George R.I.

The monarch was still Rex Imperator, King and Emperor. The sentiments expressed in the letter permeated almost every aspect of my childhood. I was ever aware that the country I found myself in, our country, had won a war. In the early years I had little enough notion of what war had entailed but we had definitely scored more than the Germans and the Japs - that was the point. I remember Dad explaining what might have happened if we had lost. The Germans would have ruled us. They would have killed or imprisoned lots of people. They liked only people who looked a certain way: fair hair and blue eyes were the thing. I had fair hair and blue eyes and, even as Dad told me this, I thought with a little air of triumph that I would probably have been what the Germans were looking for. I would have been OK. The instinct for self-preservation plotting a path to treachery.

The rear of the certificate listed important dates of the war. Had I studied it I would have learned that I had been born six weeks after the fall of Singapore, a low point in the struggle. Beneath this was a space for "My family's war record". It is blank.

It might not have been. At the beginning of the war the country expected a German bombing campaign and each firm had to have a rescue team. Dad went first aid training in the evening for several weeks before the authorities realised that in an emergency he lived too far away to get quickly enough to Organ's yard where the lorry and equipment were kept. He was stood down. In the event, while bombers were often heard flying over the city, Oxford was not bombed. The story I was told as a boy was that there was an agreement that if the Allies did not bomb Heidelberg the Germans would not bomb Oxford. Heidelberg was not bombed but I can find no firm evidence of any such quid pro quo. Another tale is that Hitler intended to make Oxford his capital after invading but this is again, I think, just speculation. It is just possible that there was a specific reason for the city's escape, for unlike Heidelberg, Oxford did have legitimate military targets: Morris Motors was given over to aircraft building and repairs during the war; Osberton Radiators made parts for the Merlin engines that powered Spitfires and Hurricanes.

At the outset of the war Dad assumed he would be called up, so, without telling his wife, he volunteered for the army with the aim of getting into the regiment of his choice, the Royal Engineers. The nation told him he was in a reserved occupation and declined his offer. He became a fire watcher in charge of a small group of Kingston Road neighbours, who practised putting out fires with stirrup pumps and empty buckets. When the bombs didn't come he patrolled less than assiduously. Hettie would hear the warning siren and wake him up. "I heard it," he would say. "It's the all clear, it's all right," and go back to sleep.

A new aerodrome was to be built at Grove, near Wantage and Dad was offered a foreman's job there. This was fortunate, for at the age of 34 he was now summoned for his service medical. He passed A1 and returned home looking "glum", according to him, "frightened" according to my mother. Call up papers duly arrived and he prepared to leave but, without his asking, his employers secured deferment, needing him at the new aerodrome. Grove was intended for Bomber Command but in 1943 became a home of the American Ninth Air Force in Britain. Even if Dad had been called to the colours and perhaps been sent overseas or killed, there would still be a me, since I was already conceived. It was while he was working at Grove that I was born in January 1942.

The Home Guard now came knocking. Dad was working long hours at the aerodrome, which was nearly twenty miles from his home. Once again, he was excused. Then, in 1944, Organs was directed to repair bomb-damaged houses in London and Dad was to be part of the workforce. When he explained his departure to the middle-class woman who was convenor of the fire-watchers she replied, "Most noble of you, Mr Wyatt, most noble."

He went first to Kingston-on-Thames, travelling with his elder brother Frank, who had won the Military Medal and bar in the previous war and was confident he could sort things. "You stick with me, Bas. I'll dig us a slit trench and we'll be OK." They were billeted in a school and on arrival Frank told Dad to wait while he went for a reconnaissance. He was soon back and said to bring the cases to the headmaster's room which the two of them could take over and share. Dad was chuffed to have his quarters arranged so satisfactorily. He

reckoned without the brute instincts of some Wyatts. An hour later
Frank was back: "Take your bloody stuff out of here, Bas. Bill Bott
is coming in with me." No wonder Basil had demanded of Organs
that he be in charge of his own site with no interference from his
elder brother.

They were seven to a classroom, though often sleeping in an
underground air raid shelter. Living arrangements could have been
much worse. There were no chores, their food was cooked for them
and came with extra rations. Much of the damage to houses had
been caused by the V1 flying bombs, doodlebugs. I used to listen in
awe to Dad's descriptions of them: the straightness of their flight,
the flame at the rear and how when their buzzing sound suddenly
cut out you knew they would then dive to earth. The first time he
heard the warning klaxon he was working on a roof and instead of
climbing down to seek cover he thought he'd stay and take a look
at one of these flying bombs. He foolishly did and was shaken up
badly by the force of the explosion, lucky not to be hurt. The injuries
that he did sustain came when he was inspecting a badly damaged
roof and a ceiling joist gave way so he crashed through to the floor
below injuring his back and chest.

So I could, I suppose, fill in the blank space on the certificate,
"Father volunteered - rejected (reserved occupation). Rescue team
- stood down. Fire watcher - occasional; Called up - deferred
(reserved occupation); Home Guard - stood down. Repaired bomb
damage in the capital as V1 rockets fell." But I will leave it as it is.

My only firm memory of the war itself is climbing with Dad
to the top floor of the house when he put the blackout blinds away,
there being no longer any need for them. Either the war had ended
or it was evident the Germans would be sending no more bombers.
In the Oxford of my childhood no bomb damage testified that we

had been at war but there was no missing the men in royal blue suits, some with crutches and a flapping trouser leg. These I was solemnly informed were wounded soldiers. There were also the many Americans stationed near Oxford, both soldiers and airmen. I associate them with loose, pale blue suits, a colour no Englishman ever wore, and an easy, assured air. I knew they were better off, that they had helped our country out with money, ships and guns. I and other children would approach and ask, "Got any gum, chum?" and were usually rewarded. Chewing gum, unknown at the sweet shop, said "American" as kilts said "Scotsman".

On the wall of the living room hung one of our few pictures, a reproduced line drawing of the nation's hero, Winston Churchill. My parents were firm Conservatives and impressed upon us how much we owed him. He was the great "Without whom…" When talking of the war Dad often slipped into a military mode, peppering us with quotes of songs or materiel from the radio or building site. "Thank you very much for those few kind words, lady. But don't forget Berlin," or a favourite, "Win 'em and wear 'em, like the soldiers do wooden legs."

National pride, victorious Britain, valiant Churchill all flourished in soil well fertilised by my early reading. I was given Highroads of History, second book for Christmas when I was six. It comprised stories from British history from King Arthur to the First World War, illustrated by reproductions of mostly Victorian paintings. In "Slave Boys at Rome" I read of a slave market where "stood three little English boys. Their faces were pink and white, their eyes were blue and they had long yellow hair". A monk asked the "keen, hard faced slave dealer, 'To what people do these boys belong?' 'They are 'Angles'. 'Angles!' cried the monk; 'They should be angels, they are so beautiful.'"

I glowed. Other chapters told of Hereward the Wake, brave rebel against William of Normandy and of the death of bad King William the Red in the New Forest (I longed to see the Rufus Stone, supposed site of the oak which deflected the arrow to the king and eventually persuaded my parents to take me there). A chapter described the Children's Crusade marching vainly towards the Holy Land only for most to die on the way or in shipwrecks, the survivors sold into slavery in Africa.

I have always been wary of big ideas and visionary schemes. Perhaps it started here. Our noble role in India featured in The Black Hole of Calcutta when an Indian prince imprisoned 145 British men and one woman in a stifling room twenty feet square so that only 23 emerged alive come morning: "When the people in England heard the news they were very angry." Again, in Jessie's Dream at the siege of Lucknow, "Outside are the cruel natives who have risen against their British masters," then the sound of the bagpipes, "We're saved; We're saved." The propaganda continued, "I have already told you how we won Canada and India, the two chief British countries across the sea. You know how our soldiers had to fight hard for them. Now let me tell you the story of South Africa, which we also won by war." Tracks were being laid here. We could do no wrong. "When things were at their worst the British nation roused itself."

A second book from that time was The History Highway, more international with chapters on the Wooden Horse, Romulus and Remus, Alexander the Great and Joan of Arc but there was ample space for Richard the Lionheart, Dick Whittington, Sir Walter Raleigh and Nelson. I loved history and when we acquired a car Dad drove us out to see the Rollright Stones in North Oxfordshire and the legendary sites on the Berkshire Downs my teacher Mr

Cox had told us about, the ancient track of the Ridgeway, Wayland's Smithy, where an invisible smith would shoe your horse, and the Blowing Stone, with which King Alfred summoned his warriors. I liked the fact that you could touch these physical elements of history and know that people had lived their lives around them. I was tantalised by the certain knowledge that the past had happened and yet it remained elusive and impossible to retrieve.

After the war, many of us children grew up with a certain cast of mind about the country we were born into. The atlas showed the lands of the British Empire in red. Vast areas of the earth were ruled by our tiny red island. A boy could not help but be proud as a son of this soil. Mr Cox explained gravely how the imprimatur "Made in England" was recognised the whole world over as the signifier of quality. "Made in Japan", on the other hand, denoted rubbish, tat and imitation. (We called them "Japs", of course; the Germans were "Huns" and in comics "Krauts".) Meanwhile, on the other side of the globe, the company that was to be Sony had launched its first tape recorder and Panasonic made its first 17-inch television set.

The glory continued, so it seemed, with British aircraft triumphs. I followed news of the early flights of the Canberra jet bomber (three are still in service with NASA), the delta winged Avro 707 bomber and another glamourous delta wing, the Gloster Javelin all-weather fighter. Test pilots were heroes. Group Captain John Cunningham, an ex-fighter pilot, flew the first jet airliner, the Comet, so sleek and beautiful in shape but which went on to a string of fatal accidents. Another decorated fighter pilot, Squadron Leader Neville Duke, flew the Hawker Hunter in which he held the world air speed record. I grieved for John Derry, the first Briton to break the speed of sound, and the test pilot of the DH 110 who died at the Farnborough Air Show in September 1952 when his aircraft broke up, killing him, his co-pilot and 29 spectators. Even then the heart could swell, for extraordinarily the show went on. Immediately after the disastrous crash Derry's friend Neville Duke took up his Hawker Hunter to give a display and demonstrate what Brits were made of.

The other great pilot of the time was Dan Dare, square jawed, crinkly eye-browed, futuristic space captain from the front page of the Eagle comic. He was the first person to fly to Venus, base of his long-time foe the Mekon, green, bulbous headed leader of the Treens. I took the Eagle from its first issue. It was launched with great publicity as an upmarket comic with better quality paper and dramatic colour printing, the centre spread a cutaway diagram of a plane, railway engine, car, ship or some other machine. There was an improving air to the whole enterprise but I simply lapped up the contents, PC 49, Riders of the Range and Tommy Walls. This last was an advertising strip in which Tommy pulled off great feats of rescue and the like when he made the magic Walls Ice Cream sign, a W, with his thumbs and index fingers. Even further upmarket was The Children's Newspaper, which was exactly what it sounds like and pretty dull. It was unknown to me until Phil and Jim school entered a team in an Oxford Top of the Form competition for which the questions would all be based on a couple of editions of this publication. I dutifully mugged up. We were beaten by Wheatley County School but I secured my first newspaper cutting as second top scorer with six points.

Mostly my comic reading was the Beano (Lord Snooty and his pals), Dandy (Desperate Dan and Aunt Aggie's cow pie), Radio Fun with its cast of wireless stars such as Pet Clarke, Jimmy Jewel and Ben Warriss, Issy Bonn, Arthur English and Big Hearted Arthur Askey, and Film Fun, which featured Laurel and Hardy, Old Mother

Riley, Joe E. Brown and Terry Thomas in its strips. Western comics each carried stories of one B-movie western star. My favourites were fresh faced Monte Hale, "six feet six with a six shooter", Rocky Lane and Lash LaRue, not that I ever saw any of the films and doubt that I realised their adventures were enacted anywhere but in the illustrated pages. The admirable Classics Illustrated series introduced me to the classics. I consumed the comic strip versions of Tale of Two Cities, Gulliver's Travels, Last of the Mohicans, Two Years Before the Mast, The Three Musketeers and more.

I began to read the newspaper proper, the sports pages at least. We had the Daily Express delivered. Its star sports writer was Desmond Hackett whose trade mark ploy was to bet his brown bowler hat that something would or would not happen. My first memory of news is the map of Korea that featured on the front page in the months following the outbreak of the Korean War in 1950. The front line was marked in bold across the peninsula and moved south until it described just a corner. This was bad. Nevertheless, British heroes showed me that the gallantry of the World War lived on. The brave stand of the Glorious Gloucesters in the face of a mighty onslaught from the Chinese army and the courage of Bill Speakman VC shone out from the pages of the Express. I could cling to these as the Commies drove us south. At one time the News of the World was present in the house. I just remember the density of print and the long thin columns, eight I think across the page. Then it was there no longer, cancelled no doubt when I began to show an interest in the stories of errant vicars, predatory scoutmasters and "vice" raids.

Mum used to call me a bookworm but looking back I think that was just because I read books at all. Mum always referred to her magazines, Home Chat, Woman's Own and so on, as "my books".

Dad wasn't a reader and worked all hours. In later life he did buy two books, both investigations into the Masons, whom he suspected of cronyism and sly dealing. I remember his reactions, "This is a bloody carry-on. They're all in it for what they can get."

Among the first books my parents read to me was The Tale of Mr Tootleoo, a charming story, told in rhyme with landscape illustrations, of a shipwrecked sailor and his life with the Cockyolly birds. The cover was plain with a red embossed medallion showing the portly Mr Tootleoo dancing a hornpipe. I had books of the Daily Express' Rupert Bear strip and lots of the Little Grey Rabbit stories by Alison Uttley, illustrated by Margaret Tempest. Modest, capable Grey Rabbit lived with lolloping, vainglorious but kindly Hare and the attention seeking Squirrel in a cottage with the steepest gable imaginable. They were cosy, funny tales. In infants' school, we performed a little play based on one of the books in which I played Hare to Valerie Gardiner's Grey Rabbit. Valerie Gardiner, who had silvery blond hair, was my favourite in the class. She went off to the girls' school and was last glimpsed from afar a few years later playing football with some boys. In those days this made her a "tomboy".

When I started to read proper story books the power of fiction captured me. I lived every twist of Black Beauty's life, shocked and reassured in turn, crying at the death of Ginger. In The Wind in the Willows, I wondered with Mole at the river skills of Ratty, I laughed at the preposterous Toad and admired the standoffish but noble Badger. I lost myself in the bravery and self-sufficiency of Bevis. These were three worlds foreign to me. I was never around horses and knew no-one who was; I was never around boats; country animals were exotic to me. I was the least brave and self-sufficient of boys. Not in those pages, though.

I had the odd Enid Blyton book but my great love was the Lone Pine series by Malcolm Saville. These provided the perfect childhood adventures. The stories were set in a real landscape, the Shropshire hills, complete with maps; the children explore alone and foil both spies and thieves; the central characters provided, in the young twins Dickie and Mary, children one could identify with and smile at, in elder brother David a strong leader to look up to and in Peter (Petronella) a "big girl" to admire, whose relationship with David was a boy-girl friendship growing into understated romance. Even as I write about them now I feel the hairs on the back of my neck rising. No books ever are as all-embracing in their intensity as those read as a child.

I bought the first edition of Charles Buchan's Football Monthly in 1951 and took it for years afterwards. Its annual was added to the others which accumulated in these years, Raymond Glendenning's Book of Sport for Boys, Stanley Matthews' Football Album, Boys' Book of All Sports, F.A. Book for Boys. You get the idea.

Photos of sports stars Freddie Mills the boxer, Johnny Leach, table tennis champion and, best of all, Denis Compton striding to the wicket, featured in a favourite, the Daily Mail 1950 Annual. It comprised illustrated stories, puzzles, short articles and colour photos, notably of Princess Elizabeth and Prince Philip's wedding, and a spread on fruits of the hedgerow. Among the hawthorn, blackberry, sloe and lords and ladies I paid close attention to the Deadly Nightshade and Woody Nightshade, studying the differentiating descriptions and with forensic care, for of the former, "Only one berry can cause death to a small child". Thereafter, I examined every hedgerow.

An article with black and white photos headed "Stars of Tomorrow" was about the Italia Conti stage school. Photos of the school's production of Where the Rainbow Ends included one of the chief fairy, an attractive girl with short curly hair, pretending to play a fairy pipe as she sat on a toadstool, her transparent flowing vestment hanging loose, one long bare leg touching the ground, the other raised and pointed in the air. Many times I went back to this strangely alluring photograph, gazing at it without ever quite knowing why.

I knew why I enjoyed the biographies and memoirs of the war which tumbled forth in the early fifties. They showed how strong and brave "we" had been in the face of danger and cruelty. The Dam Busters told the now well-known story of 617 Squadron, led by dashing Wing Commander Guy Gibson in its raids on the Ruhr dams. The Colditz Story and Escape or Die recounted stories of daring escape attempts from the fortress prison and other prisoner of war camps. Boldness Be My Friend, Evader and Where Bleed the Many were individual tales of resourceful escapers and resistance fighters. Down in the Drink stirred me with accounts of RAF air crews who were shot down over the sea. Cheshire VC was the biography of the extraordinary Group Captain Leonard Cheshire VC, DSO and two Bars, DFC who was awarded his Victoria Cross not for one act of valour but for sustained courage and leadership in more than 100 bombing raids over Germany. He had been to the Dragon School, they who had bowled us out for sixteen, but he could be forgiven that as he was a local boy and a hero. All these proved just how fortunate I was to be British even as I doubted I was forged from quite the same metal as Cheshire and co. The Naked Island left a different mark. Russell Braddon recorded his terrible years as a prisoner of the Japanese in Changi gaol and on the Burma Railway. I lay awake trying to imagine what beriberi would be like with liquid swilling about in my swollen legs. Dysentery and permanent diarrhoea I could visualise. It would be some years before I could think about the Japanese as other than brutes who tore out fingernails and beat starving men.

Many of these books were turned into films. Through watery eyes I watched Jack Hawkins, aiming for a German submarine, drop depth charges among shipwrecked British sailors waving and hoping for rescue in The Cruel Sea. Friends and I would afterward look serious and croak, "It's the war, Number One. The whole bloody war." The licence to say "bloody" was very grown-up. This was followed by The Colditz Story, Above Us the Waves and Cockleshell Heroes in which I puzzled even then at the very unmilitary American José Ferrer commanding Royal Marine Commandoes. And, of course, walking tall from the cinema at the end of The Dam Busters, head held high, lump in my throat and Eric Coates' march ringing in my ears.

There were five cinemas in Oxford. The Ritz at Gloucester Green was the largest and grandest. When I was in my teens I would sometimes go with Mum and sit in the huge balcony with a box of chocolates. The Regal was another enormous cinema but this was up Cowley Road and off my beat until much later. I often went to the Super, now the Odeon, in Magdalen Street, handy for the buses to North Oxford, and less often to the Electra in Queen Street. The Scala in Walton Street was closest to home but deemed to be a fleapit and "for the undergrads".

My first ever film was The Wizard of Oz but I was so frightened by the opening black and white sequence of the tornado that I had to be taken out. I was much affected by what must have been a re-release of The Four Feathers, a tale of British soldiers fighting the natives in Egypt. Again, here were brave chaps defending the Empire. The scene that haunted me was when the sun-blinded Ralph Richardson staggered through the blazing desert as vultures circled overhead. I asked Dad what vultures did. He told me. I was shaken, too, by the upending of everything I thought right when Jack Warner as PC George Dixon was shot and fatally wounded by the young crook, Dirk Bogarde, in The Blue Lamp. This was in my England. Dixon's young protégé did catch the killer which restored the natural order but, for me, only sort of.

By the time I was ten I went frequently to the pictures with friends. Most films we wanted to see were "U" certificate, suitable for all audiences, but some were "A" certificate, to which children were only admitted if accompanied by an adult. For these we would hang about outside the cinema and ask strangers, usually men, "Will you take us in please?" There was no secrecy about it. We would give them our money and they would buy our tickets. That was that. Once inside we didn't have to sit with our enabler and none of them ever tried to sit by me.

We took little notice of programme times and often went in with the main film underway, quickly picking up the thread. An essential task was to spot whether murdered or other dead bodies were still breathing. "Look, there! The man with the spear, you can his chest moving." A little triumph to congratulate ourselves that we'd seen through the whole elaborate charade. As if we ever thought they really were killing people. Then there was an interval - "Our sales staff will now visit all parts of the theatre" - and a black and white Pathé News, upbeat, often jingoistic, coverage of topical new stories, the stentorian commentary making every item sound either grimly threatening - "Day and night the watch goes on…" - or reassuringly satisfactory - "These youngsters show they have inherited the spirit that breeds greatness.". This was followed by the supporting feature, often true life British crime stories, introduced portentously by Edgar Lustgarten, crime writer and former barrister. Eventually, the main picture began and when it reached the point we recognised one of us would whisper,

"This is where we came in."

"Yes, let's go," and we would make our way out to catch the bus home for tea.

Adventure films were my first love after a bad moment in Robin Hood and His Merrie Men I think it was when a character was made to walk over red hot coals. As soon as I spotted that coming I went out to the Gents until the nasty stuff was over. The first star I idolised was Stewart Granger in The Prisoner of Zenda, brave, selfless and riding into the sunset at the end: "Goodbye, Fritz, we fought a good fight." "Goodbye, Englishman. Fate doesn't always make the right man king." He was even more dashing as the eponymous swordsman in Scaramouche, which introduced me to Janet Leigh, she of the rosebud mouth, wide set eyes, glowing skin and formidable breasts, to whom I would have pledged my troth. I followed her in Prince Valiant, then The Black Shield of Falworth and Houdini, both with Tony Curtis, her husband, "the happiest marriage in Hollywood", so I read. I didn't mind this news as she was like the attractive big sister of a friend, beautiful but unreachable. Houdini set me reading about the great magician, especially his activities as a scourge of spiritualists and fake mediums. I began to learn some simple magic tricks.

Janet Leigh was not alone, for I had melted before Elizabeth Taylor in the film of Ivanhoe and soon I had a taste for musicals beginning with Because You're Mine, with Mario Lanza, and Showboat. In a trice came Calamity Jane and I was struck again by the blond and husky voiced Doris Day, who reminded me of my older cousin Anne, also a singer. I didn't miss any of the great

American musicals made into films in the fifties and developed a tendresse for another milk- and corn-fed American blonde, Shirley Jones, in Oklahoma.

There were the westerns, too. My heart was tugged at the end of Shane when Alan Ladd rode away and the boy's cry echoed, "Shane! Shane! Come back!" I welled up, too, at the collection of O. Henry stories in Full House, ending with the poor couple who give each other prized gifts for Christmas. He sells his watch in order to buy a beautiful tiara for her long, beautiful hair; she cuts and sells her hair to buy a chain for his pocket watch. The biggest emotional punch came from On the Waterfront. I sought to hold back tears at the end as Marlon Brando, the longshoreman and ex-boxer, staggered bloodedly and nobly toward the dock in defiance of the corrupt union boss. The film was the harshest depiction of the brutality and unfairness of the grown-up world that I had seen and left a deep impression. And it had Eva Marie Saint.

I was soon hooked on the pictures, as we always called them. (I was quite put out and thought it was showing off when the great Guy Gibson VC wrote about going to "the movies" in his book, Enemy Coast Ahead.) Mum's weekly help in the house was now Elsie, who worked part time as an usherette at the Scala cinema and subscribed to the sepia-coloured weekly fan magazine, Picturegoer, copies of which she passed on to me. I pored over it and the annual arrived at Christmas with articles on dancers Marge and Gower Champion from Showboat, and Janette Scott, the pretty pigtailed British actress a few years older than me whom I had seen in The Galloping Major. No Christmas in the fifties would pass without the Picturegoer or Film Review annual.

At home, entertainment was the wireless. Our set, about a foot high and eighteen inches wide, was a significant presence in the living room. It had two dials, one for volume, the other moving an indicator left or right along the illuminated tuning panel. BBC Light, BBC Home and BBC Third were marked along with Daventry, Hilversum, Prague, Paris and other distant transmitters.

Sometimes the whole family would all listen to, say, Variety Bandbox with Arthur English as comic compere and a big band or, a favourite of Dad's, Henry Hall's Guest Night. Its signature tune, "Here's to the Next Time" was followed by a prissy introduction from the host, "This is Henry Hall and tonight is my guest night." I thought he was trying to sound posh. Mum and I listened to Workers' Playtime in the holidays and when the comic sang at the end, as he always did, we'd agree as if it were a surprise that he had a very nice voice. We all liked Ray's A Laugh, a domestic comedy with Ted Ray and Kitty Bluett, The Charlie Chester Show with its silly songs, "Down in the jungle living in a tent, Better than a prefab - no rent," and Educating Archie, popular at the time but which was the oddity of a ventriloquist act on the radio, Peter Brough and his dummy Archie Andrews. The young Julie Andrews played Archie's girlfriend. We shared a weekly frisson with The Man in Black, the dark and frightening voice of actor Valentine Dyall reading a horror story. On Saturday evening we clustered to hear In Town Tonight, in effect an early chat show which opened with a jaunty orchestral march into which bled sounds of traffic and Londoners talking, just catching a cockney woman's voice saying "Violets, lovely violets lady," before a man cried "Stop!", the sounds of traffic ceased and the announcer began: "Once more we stop the mighty roar of London's traffic and, from the great crowds, we bring you some of the interesting people who have come by land, sea and air to be In Town Tonight."

For the nightly fifteen-minute serial Dick Barton Special Agent, I would huddle close to the set, gripped as Dick found himself in yet another apparently impossible spot and called for his sidekicks: "Help… Jock… Snowy… Aaagh!" Up came the thrilling music: dum diddly um, dum diddly um, dum diddly um dum, dum dum dum… a cliff-hanger every evening. My ear was close to the set for other shows I listened to more than my parents, the ground breaking Take It From Here with the continuing saga of the dysfunctional Glum family, overbearing Mr Glum played by a wicked sounding Jimmy Edwards, and the never ending engagement of the dim Ron, Dick Bentley, and humdrum Eth, June Whitfield. Like another favourite comedy Much Binding in the Marsh, TIFH had not a signature tune but a song,

> Take it from here, don't go away when you can take it from here.
> Don't go away when you can join in the fun, now the show has begun…

A bit defensive in retrospect, but I sang along then and do now. Two other shows for me - and school friends - rather than Mum and Dad were The Goon Show and Hancock's Half Hour. We sought to amuse each other with our versions of the funny voice Goon characters Eccles, Bloodnok and Bluebottle, and of the stammering introduction to H-H-Hancock.

Radio was the only source of music. I joined in with the cheery voices of Rosemary Clooney, "Come On-a My House", and Guy Mitchell, "My Truly, Truly Fair". When I think of the radio at that time I think of the Stargazers singing group who were regulars on the Light Programme. They introduced themselves with a jingle, "The Stargazers aaaa Rontheair" and had a line in novelty songs:

Twenty tiny fingers, twenty tiny toes;
Two angel faces, each with a turned up nose.
One looks like mummy, with a cute little curl on top;
and the other one's got a big bald spot exactly like his pop,
pop, pop, pop-a-dop, pop, pop, Pop-pop.

This was a hit record! The Saturday morning record request show for children was eclectic and introduced its listeners to the Sabre Dance by Khachaturian, Largo al Factotum from The Barber of Seville, Radetzky March by Johann Strauss, the Halleluiah Chorus along with "Nellie the Elephant", "The Runaway Train", "Three Little Fishes Swam Over the Dam" and "Big Hearted Arthur" Askey singing

Oh, what a wonderful thing to be,
A healthy grown up busy, busy bee;
Whiling away all the passing hours,
Pinching all the pollen from the cauliflowers.

And then came television. One day early in 1949 Dad drove the family to Newbury to visit Auntie Phyl and Uncle Ron. As we drew up outside their house Ron came to the door to greet us.

"How did you know we had arrived?" Dad asked.

"Ahaa! Come inside and see," replied Ron, who ran an electrical business. He led us to their sitting room where stood a console model television set. There were only around half a million sets in the United Kingdom at the time and this was the first we had seen. He explained and we soon saw for ourselves that when a car passed the house or drew up outside, the screen responded with a noisy blizzard of white spots and jagged white lines, destroying the picture. This seemed a bit of a difficulty for the new device but it was outweighed by the wonder of moving pictures. In any event it was soon compulsory for cars to be fitted with suppressors banishing this interference. We returned to Newbury on a never to be forgotten day that April to watch the FA Cup Final live, Billy Wright leading Wolves to a 3-1 win over Leicester City.

A couple of years later we had our own television, a twelve-inch screen KB table model. It was installed in the first floor lounge at 15 Kingston Road, the room in which any of our rare entertaining took place. Children's programmes included the marionette Muffin the Mule which I could watch with my younger brother David, the slapstick character Mr Pastry, Whirligig with another puppet Mr Turnip, Johnny Morris telling stories as The Hot Chestnut Man, and the western series The Lone Ranger and Hopalong Cassidy. The announcer for children's programmes was the appealingly posh Jennifer Gay who looked as if she were at her own birthday party, with Alice band, breathy voice and impeccable enunciation. She could not be mine but I think I wondered if I could find one like her.

Our magical new contraption brought sport, too. The BBC showed amateur football on Saturday afternoons, Barnet versus Hendon and the like, the players tiny grey blurs when they moved to the far side of the pitch. In summer, I could hurry back from school to watch the after tea session of test matches. The evening entertainment we watched as a family appears quaint in retrospect: Café Continental, a variety show set in a French cabaret of the sort BBC producers must have patronised or believed their middle-class viewers did; Kaleidoscope, which engaged a "viewer-competitor" on the telephone in a quiz after a brief montage of shots of the viewer's home town taken "by our cameraman Fotheringay" - much excitement when one week it was Oxford and we saw shots of a road near ours. We liked the family serials, the Appleyards, and better still The Grove Family, the father of which was, like Dad, a small builder. When hungry we adopted the grumpy northern grandma's complaint, "I'm faint for lack of nourishment." The comedians we liked were the large, blustering and apparently inebriated Fred Emney, the naughty schoolboy like Benny Hill and the physical comedy of the droll Max Wall, who gyrated at the piano and in funny walks in black tights with mad professor hair. I later liked the story that he was banned from television after taking off his trilby, making a groove in the crown with his stiffened hand, showing this to the camera before gazing at it wistfully and commenting, "Well, you never know. Someone might fancy a bit of a nibble."

Early television revelled in its ability to cover live events. I loved Trooping the Colour as did Dad who would adopt a military pose and exclaim, "Halt the bays and steady the greys and let the Oxford and Bucks come through." I remember Mum asking, "What regiment was old so and so, Jean's dad, in? Was that the guards?" "No," replied Dad, "He was a short arse." Anything with enough flummery was televised by the BBC. Richard Dimbleby, the nation's guide on these occasions, would make much of royal coaches stopping at Temple Bar to request permission of the Lord Mayor to venture further and so on. It all sounded so important to my young ears.

Our KB television set never went wrong. It was manufactured before any thought of a second channel so when ITV began in 1955 we remained a BBC only family and were so until well after I had left home. The BBC shut down programmes at six o'clock for the hour-long "toddlers' truce", the thinking being that parents could then put small children to bed. This was ended soon after the introduction of ITV. To fill the gap, the BBC introduced an early evening magazine programme which set their programmes on a new, jauntier path. I was entranced from the start. Tonight was introduced by Cliff Michelmore with a band of characterful reporters, Fyfe Robertson and Macdonald Hastings from Picture Post magazine, Alan Whicker and Kenneth Allsop from Fleet Street. This was yet to come.

Even further ahead was a BBC series about the press I produced with Ken Allsop. This brought the terrible day when he failed to arrive in London for the studio. When it was evident that something was wrong I rang the Dorset police to alert them. Ken had committed suicide.

Dad, David and I imitating
an advertisement at
Highcliffe.

8
A BIT OF FUN

When my brother David was little we could squeeze the family into the cabin of the Austin 7 pickup. Dad must have kept this for work but I remember more journeys in the round nosed Morris 8, which carried the four of us more comfortably. Cars were in short supply and it was Dad's brother Bill who found a route to this one, purchased second hand from a director at Morris's. My parents liked to go for what they called a "ride round" on a Sunday. This would be a spin in the countryside, usually north or west of Oxford always ending with a stop at a pub, Shepherds Hall near Witney, The Fox at Boars Hill, The Evenlode at Eynsham and other favourites, where David and I would stay outside in the car with a packet of crisps and a bottle of lemonade.

Sometimes there was a specific destination. I loved inventing hiding and escape games in the scrubby woodland on Boars Hill, concluding with a climb up the mound. A favourite spot for a picnic, always tea never lunch, was the top of the Chiltern escarpment near Christmas Common, where I could run down the steep incline scattering the uncountable numbers of pre-myxomatosis rabbits into their warrens. Another was the Berkshire and Lambourn Downs, all grass in those days and where there was hope of glimpsing a racehorse. In spring, we picked wildflowers. We knew special places for primroses, then for bluebells and in late spring buttercups, all of which were gathered in shameless abundance.

We drove for tea to Mum's friends from service, Anne and her husband Range, at Hedges Farm in Oakley. We would have eaten a proper Sunday lunch but an enormous tea would await us - sandwiches, homemade cakes, scones and, uniquely in my world, double cream. We made an expedition "to London", actually to Auntie Edie, Mum's cousin, who lived in Chingford, Essex, but Chingford like Auntie Glad's home in Borehamwood, Hertfordshire, counted as London from as far west as Oxfordshire. On one of the rare excursions to Chingford the windscreen of our little Morris was smashed by boys with a catapult on Western Avenue. There was nothing to be done but finish the journey and return with the cold air blasting through the car. Auntie Edie was a welcome if very occasional visitor to us and to Leafield. She made a great fuss of David and me had did jolly things like writing down her tip for the Grand National, "Hoof Hearted". She never married and ran a cake shop in Station Road, Chingford. I sense there might have been a woman friend but can't be sure. She and Mum like to slip into Leafield talk, "them lot be as poor as Job" and, "I can't compass with it."

We paid Sunday calls on Uncles Stan and John in Leafield and on Auntie Phyl and Uncle Ron in Newbury. We also made Saturday trips to Newbury for the races, always I think flat rather than jump racing. I would pick a horse from the race card and Dad would put on a small bet for me. On an early visit, it could even have been my first, I picked five winners in the six races and from then on there was then no looking back. I devised a simplistic method, backing horses that had been third and second in their latest outings believing this to indicate an improving animal. So it might have been but my naivety made no allowance for the standard of the races nor the changing weight carried by horses in handicaps. I learned about this and my study became closer. I recall plotting the positions I anticipated every Derby runner would be in after the first two furlongs, at the top of the hill, at Tattenham Corner and at the finishing post. I saw every race as a puzzle. If I accumulated enough information and concentrated hard I would be able to figure out the result. It did not occur to me for many years that there is no result until the race is run and that a multitude of variables impossible to anticipate would affect what happened. Your selection, your bet, was not the answer to the puzzle but just a possible outcome at given odds. I soon knew the colours of major owners: chocolate and green for the Aga Khan, white and maroon for Major Holliday, pale blue with pink sash for Lord Astor and more. I read the *Daily Express'* racing correspondents, Clive Graham, "The Scout", and Peter O'Sullevan. We acquired a horse racing game called Escalado. You turned a handle to vibrate a long green canvas course, the vibrations moving lead model horses and jockeys from the start to a finish line. You bet on the result.

We must have driven to our early holidays by the sea, in places I have never been to since, popular in their day. I know we went to Cliftonville and Clacton-on-Sea but have no memory of them. Of Leigh-on-Sea I remember only wallowing happily in the mud. In 1949 Dad and Uncle Ron bought a wooden holiday chalet called "Rusticana" on Naish Farm estate near Highcliffe-on-Sea in Dorset now, Hampshire then. They built an extension largely of asbestos, which gave a decent sitting area. and there was room for both families to be there together, though we mostly went separately. The sanitary arrangements, an Elsan chemical toilet, were primitive, nothing more than a metal can with lavatory seat, into which we emptied our bowels adding some strong disinfectant. It was emptied twice a week by the poo lorry we dubbed "Honey Joe".

The first year or so we drove in the pickup with David's four-wheel pram in the back, together with the bed linen and some food. With the little Morris 8 we occasionally went for the weekend. In the summer Mum, David and I were there for three or four weeks and Dad would drive down to join us on Friday evenings. David and I walked to the farm entrance excitedly competing for the first glimpse of him. Naish Farm had a shop so we could manage without a car during the week. The site had several hundred dwellings, from quite substantial wooden houses to old buses and converted railway carriages. Some were inhabited the year round. These permanent residents sported a *PR* sign and were not always at ease with the holiday makers. Owners of the converted GWR rolling stock next to Rusticana erected a tall *Keep Off the Grass* sign on the tempting green sward in front, a source of scorn on our part and not a little friction as we did not try hard to obey and even posed mockingly either side for photographs. At the centre of the whole estate was a large green on which people flew kites and pick-up games of cricket developed.

"The bungalow," as it was always referred to, provided the happiest of holidays. We could walk down the crumbling cliffs to a beach which looked out to the Isle of Wight and the Needles. There were steps but much more fun was to scramble over the blocks of clay and crumbling earth that tumbled away from the unstable edges as the land retreated. Uncle Walter, Mum's brother, had left his wife, Auntie Aggie, and she several times came on holiday with us, getting up at seven to chaperone Dave and me on these not altogether safe adventures. We spent the days on the beach, swimming, playing ball games, building sandcastles and attempting to block the little stream that ran down to the sea from the tree lined valley, Chewton Bunny as it was called. In front of the bungalow itself was a small patch of bracken, raw material for our spears and a low forest to crawl through and make camp in the middle, out of sight as we thought of grown-ups. Asbestos and bracken, both carcinogenic - no-one knew; dangerous cliffs - just good fun.

Dad loved this holiday retreat and his good spirits brought out his part remembered lines from comic monologues or building site silliness: "It wasn't the cough that carried him off it was the coffin they carried him off in" or "No one spoke in the shop and the barber kept on shaving." There might be a little dance, "Sister Mary walka like this…" We played cards, rummy mostly, and for a treat I would go with Dad to buy fish and chips in New Milton.

Then, suddenly, we went no more. Neither did we see Auntie Phyl and Uncle Ron who had been a regular presence in our lives. There had been a row. As I understand it, Dad and Ron had agreed that if one or other wished to give up the bungalow the other would buy him out at an agreed value. According to Dad, Ron assumed that our family would want to keep it and named a price. In fact, Dad was happy to relinquish it as he could see we would make less use of it when I had a busier school life at Magdalen, where there was both Saturday morning school and Saturday afternoon sport. Ron now had to pay the price he had expected Dad to pay, a blow to his pocket and his pride. He thought he had been outsmarted. The two families stopped speaking.

We still went due south to the coast as many Oxford people did. At Easter and Whitsun we stayed in a pub in Boscombe, went to church on Easter Day, played pitch and putt golf and shopped in Bournemouth at a toyshop near the Pavilion that sold the lead model knights inspired by the film of *Ivanhoe*. We drove out to the New Forest and at Whitsun took an early sea swim. In the summer one year we went for a week to Butlin's holiday camp at Pwllheli in North Wales. As a family we weren't really joiners but Dad enjoyed the knobbly knees competition, Mum the dancing, all of us the entertainment. I went to the "club" for ten to twelve year olds and felt very grown up for about two minutes when "Uncle Brian" who was in charge offered himself as our buddy: "Forget the 'uncle'. Just call me Brian." We slept in a wooden cabin and I developed asthmatic wheezing, couldn't sleep and had to get medicine from the camp doctor. Some people developed tummy trouble. "It's all the hot food," a woman on a nearby table advised knowingly. "They're not used to it."

A couple of years later sights were raised, for 1956 was the year the Wyatt family applied for their first passports and we went to Dinard in Brittany. We flew from Bournemouth to Dinan and for all the excitement generated by my expertise in test pilots, the latest aircraft and the triumphs of the Royal Air Force, I was distinctly queasy en route. It was a foretaste of RAF flights to come. The food at the hotel offered novel but not unpleasant seafood and tastes I did not experience again for many years. The French holiday was deemed a success but it was for now a solitary experiment. Whether on account of cost or because abroad had been sampled and that would do, Ilfracombe and Newquay were the destinations that followed.

A few years afterwards I cycled home from school one afternoon to see an unfamiliar car outside our house. When I went in I discovered that it was Auntie Phyl and Uncle Ron. They had dropped in unannounced. The row was over. Relations slipped back easily to the way they were. This was especially good for Mum as Phyl was the family member she felt closest to since childhood and with whom she shared her secrets. All of us were pleased. I had always loved Phyl's sense of mischief and the cosy vanilla smell of Ron's pipe tobacco that permeated their house. We could go back to spending Christmas together: Phyl urging us to dress up, "Are we going to have a bit of fun then?" and Ron writing his little plays and sketches. These were set among the dim, unfriendly folk of Fiddly Town and featured the mean Stanley Hooper and his dopey brother John, the shy, innocent Basil Wyatt, Hettie saving her money in secret and enjoying every opportunity for a little drink with Phyl, the village girl rescued from penury and grime by the author.

My parents loaded David and me with presents at Christmas, avowedly making up for the lack of them in their own childhood. We hung up not only stockings but pillowcases, two each on occasion. Santa always put an orange in the heel of the stocking. Apart from the annuals I remember boxes of toy soldiers, a cowboy outfit with elaborate cap-shooting six gun, a Meccano set and a Bayko kit of moulded plastic bricks, doors, windows and roofs and supporting steel rods which one assembled to build houses. One year when small I was given an "O" gauge electric trainset, rarer and much larger than usual train sets, bought by Dad from someone he had done work for. It was not easy to set up and operate and I had my poor father on his knees at six on Christmas morning fitting it together, examining the wires, checking the plug and testing the fuse. It was not a success and was soon replaced later by the more usual Hornby Dublo which David and I shared.

My birthday fell just after Christmas and any sport or film annual that had not appeared in my pillow case arrived then. Mum and Dad each gave me a birthday card, the early ones featuring toys or animals, then more stately ones, "To My SON", with sailing ships, globes, piles of books, even flowers and for my seventh birthday an illustration of a thatched cottage.

May the very best of luck
Be always close at hand
And make each BIRTHDAY happier
For a SON
Who's Really Grand!

Christmas also meant the pantomime at the New Theatre. We sat in the stalls. This provided a good view of the principal boy in her tights and a chance to single out one of the chorus girls for special attention. It also put one at risk at the inevitable sing-a-long scene when a couple of children were brought up on stage. This happened midway through the second half of the show and I could not relax until this dread moment was over. David was chosen one year and by doing his best made the audience laugh as he was meant to, though he could not understand why.

The New Theatre was in George Street which was "down town", the heart of the city to which I went only occasionally. My first ever memory of Oxford other than Kingston Road was when I was very small and Dad took me to the cattle market. I guess he thought I would like the animals; all I can remember is the squealing of pigs, so disturbing that I wanted to leave. The commonest purpose for going into town was being taken to the doctor whose surgery was in one of the handsome Regency terraced houses in Beaumont Street. I made many childhood visits to the quiet and revered Dr Smythe and later to the jolly, cheer you up Dr Stewart. Like most children I contracted measles, mumps and chicken pox and had to stay at home till they cleared up.

The darkest threat was infantile paralysis. I never knew of anyone who actually had it but grown-ups frowned and lowered their voices when they talked about it. I had read about the plague. This sounded similar. I got it into my head that cows pooing in the river was a likely cause. Yet we swam happily in the Thames at Port Meadow where cows pooed everywhere including the little beaches. When we children talked among ourselves about illness it was usually about appendicitis of which we knew one could swiftly die if not operated upon. We speculated on the causes. Swallowing fish bones, said one; plum stones, said another; apple pips could do it, said others. The symptoms we all thought we knew, a pain in the right side. This was a worry given how often I got the stitch from running around too much. But was it just a stitch? The other fear was lockjaw. I practised holding my mouth tight and still to see if I might survive it. Could they get food in? Not very likely. Best to avoid any cuts from stones on the Meadow, especially near the ever threatening cow poo which apparently played its part here, too. Cork we knew to be another child killer. If you swallowed even a small bit it would swell up in your stomach and in some horrible way you would die. We worried about snake bites. Adders liked sandy soil. No one had seen one but there were those who swore and hoped to die if it wasn't true that the scout and cub camp at Youlbury, near Oxford, was full of them. It was sandy up there.

Shops were the main lure of the city centre. Mum's temple was Elliston and Cavell, an old-fashioned department store in Magdalen Street, the largest shop in Oxford. It is now Debenhams. She liked the polite service and its superior air. Webbers in the High Street was a similar store from which she bought furnishing material but it didn't have quite the cachet of Ellistons. Another grand but soon to fade shop was Grimbly Hughes, high quality grocers in Cornmarket near the Carfax junction. Mum made a rare foray inside. If the centre of town was very crowded, people out shopping after the snow, perhaps, Mum would say "everyone's on the same hookem". I was taken to buy shoes at Milwards in Cornmarket, Clarks being the usually chosen brand. To check the fit I stood on the step of a wooden box contraption and pushed my feet into a hole. At my height, there were three viewing turrets through which I, Mum and the assistant could look down to see the bones of my x-rayed toes and how close they came to the edge of the shoe. This little bit of magic was the highlight of the trip. Of course, these machines were dangerous to children's feet and even more so to the assistants who stood up against them day after day. Use of them was eventually regulated and they died out. Just along Cornmarket was Fullers cake shop, source of a very occasional treat of their fluffy light walnut and coffee sponge cake. W.H. Smith was nearby and this was where Mum bought any books David or I were given. It was only when I won a prize at Magdalen College School that I discovered round the corner in Broad Street was Blackwell's, one of the great bookshops of the world.

In part this was because we were town people. Blackwell's was there for Oxford University, which was a separate country, the colleges its archipelago spread across the city. Locals who worked at the grand neoclassical printing works in Walton Street were said to work at the Clarendon Press and not the Oxford University Press. Clarendon was actually the name of the previous OUP building next to the Sheldonian Theatre in Broad Street. Neighbours let rooms to undergrads, for which they had to be registered as university lodgings. Our lodgers were not from the university. Some people around us worked as college servants, not a job my dad thought much of: "pisspot emptiers" was his term. I was aware that St John's College owned a lot of the streets and houses around Kingston Road but was hazy as to what that entailed. I never went into a college.

OXFORD BOY

I understood that Oxford was a famous place but would have put the university and Morris Motors about equal as the reason. The university's chief interest for me was dark blues sport, teams to whom I could give passionate support when they played the light blues of Cambridge. This was my Gunners versus Spurs, Liverpool versus Manchester United. There was the free first-class cricket in the Parks. The rugby team played the best sides in the land - it was an all amateur sport - just a few hundred yards up Iffley Road from my new school, and university players were often internationals soon after or even during their time as students. The varsity match against Cambridge in early December was on the new television. The running track, also on Iffley Road, was where Roger Bannister would shortly run the first four-minute mile. The football team fed the Pegasus side. Above all, there was the boat race. This seemed to stop the nation in the forties and fifties, extraordinary for a sport no-one was interested in for the remainder of the year. We were still a hat doffing country. Toffs from the two great universities ran most institutions. Their agenda became the nation's, especially if you were an Oxford boy. When we watched the Oxford boat sink in the 1951 race I felt I shared the ignominy.

A much happier sports event on television was the FA Cup Final in 1953 when Blackpool, starring the 38-year-old Stanley Matthews, came from 3-1 down with twenty minutes to play to win 4-3. This was the result for sentimental neutrals and I duly responded as the newspapers expected. A month later came the coronation of Queen Elizabeth II, another event to endorse a boy's notion that he lived in the greatest country on earth. Anticipation was high. My toy soldiers were paraded and we bought a lead model of the Coronation coach drawn by eight grey horses. I followed every element of the long and convoluted televised ceremony as Richard Dimbleby intoned the symbolism of this moment and the ancient origin of that, the chivalric tradition of this garment and the role of that worshipful officer of the household, how much the crown weighed, which jewels decorated the golden orb. Thousands of troops from Britain and the Commonwealth took part in the procession or lined the route. The young queen was the star, of course, but the Stanley Matthews role of lovable oldster was taken by Queen Salote of Tonga, a place none of us had heard of previously. Because she gamely refused to put up the roof of her carriage in spite of the rain and did lots of waving and smiling throughout the long procession, we all agreed - the family, neighbours who were watching with us, the commentators and later the newspapers - that she had been wonderful.

My Britain seemed blessed that summer. On that very morning news reached London that Brits were the first to climb Everest. A few days afterwards the queen was at Epsom to see the country's greatest jockey, Gordon Richards, assume the Stanley Matthews role in the Derby, winning it for the first time at the age of 49, his 28th and last attempt. Sentiment here was divided, for he beat the queen's horse into second place. The following week the Wyatt family went up to London to watch the royal procession to and from Trooping the Colour as it passed along the Mall - glimpsed rather than watched, perhaps, but thrilling.

The year had begun well for some of us when sweet rationing ended on 5 February. You could now buy as many sweets and as much chocolate as you had money for. After school that day, David and I walked to Mrs Porter's sweet shop in Walton Street between

Cleavers Quality House and Cape's the drapers and loaded up with Palm Toffees, Bounty Bars, Cadbury's Milk, Flying Saucers (sherbet filled coloured wafers), fruit gums and jelly babies. This wasn't the only change in our local shopping. We now had a second and closer fish and chip shop, mostly frequented for a treat after cubs and scouts. A more novel opening was a new pottery that arrived next to the newsagents. They made plates, jugs and pots glazed in hoops of off white and pale and darker greens. I recognised this as "contemporary", the word in use for modern designs of furniture and fabric, and bought a small pot for Mum's birthday. I think she liked it. I can see that I was signalling my advanced taste to myself as much as to Mum. Look, I chose china that has no flowers, horses or cottages on it! I still have the pot and I still like it. I was noticing clothes, too, togged out in a first pair of blue jeans with deep cowboy turn ups, a red plaid shirt and neckerchief, the whole ensemble inspired by Monte Hale or Roy Rogers. A prized addition was a green zip-up windcheater, a style of garment I took to be the height of modernity and, more significantly, very American. I pranced along Kingston Road in all this in a wholly un-Wyatt manner. We were resolutely not "show-offy". No one was more despised than those trying to be "the big I am". Pretension was a major sin of the loathed Masons. As Dad once put it, his voice dripping with scorn, "Old so and so was one of them, down the Kingston Road. He talked pound-noteish and lived above the bloody fish and chip shop."

This was my last summer at Phil and Jim school. A parting of the ways was nigh and Mr Gray's eleven plus ploy would dictate who my friends might be in future. Did I reflect on this at the time? I am sure that I didn't. Did I wonder if more boys than the two of us going to Magdalen had been helped? No. Did I even wonder if I deserved to go? No, again. It had all been decided. Like most children, I lived in the present. Alan Whitaker was going to Southfield. Alan was a tall, curly haired and good-hearted friend who more than any of us had looked forward to the excitement of Coronation Day. Alas, the day before he fell heavily off apparatus at a recreation ground breaking his leg so badly that he spent the great day in hospital and was left with a limp. I remained friends with him and we played together in the holidays for some years, he building model aeroplanes as I devised interesting ways of blowing them up with fireworks. We even dug a tunnel in our new garden and kitted it out as if we were wartime escapees. Neil Butler who lived a few doors away went to Cheney. Jeremy Taylor moved away. Tony Belcher, my best playground galloping chum, along with Andy Stephens and Clifford Turrill, went to the City of Oxford High School and I hardly saw them thereafter. Looking back this may seem odd but they had new friends, as did I. Our families were acquaintances not friends. While we might sometimes have tea in a friend's home, it was never lunch, and no one ever stayed over. I didn't sleep in a friend's house until I went to a twenty-first party at university.

In the 1950s the end of the summer holidays coincided with St Giles' Fair. This is a huge event for Oxford people, closing off the wide street of St Giles', the main route north from the centre of the city. It takes place on the Monday and Tuesday following the first Sunday after 1 September, St Giles' day. School term began on the Wednesday. On the Sunday evening our family ritual was to walk from Kingston Road to watch the roundabouts, booths, stalls and helter-skelter being erected, the work usually well advanced by then. My parents would bump into people they knew, people "who used to spit in our blacking". "Who was that Dad?"

"That's old codshead."

We would look out for new attractions, identify old favourites, debate whether the fair was bigger this year and conclude with a drink at The Horse and Jockey or Victoria Arms.

On the Monday afternoon, I went with friends wary, not scared, of the faster and swirlier rides but desperate to look confident and racing driver-like on the bumping cars, casual on the galloping horses, loftily amused by the frights of the ghost train. Our favourite sideshow was the boxing booth at which challengers were recruited from the crowd to fight the resident champ. It was quite expensive, a lot of waiting about was part of it and we would endlessly argue about whether or how much it was all fixed. It was real boxing, though, and we were close and could hear the punches land. We liked the flea circus where the professor picked up the tiny performers with tweezers, attached a parasol and had them walk along a trapeze wire. On one of the evenings Mum and Dad took us, pushing our way through the crowd as darkness fell, the lights dazzling us, the music making it hard for us to hear each other. Not so hard that we could not ask for and get candy floss and toffee apples. For some reason, not hot dogs. These were a recent American novelty so enticing that one friend would buy them at the fair to take home and heat up the following day or even later. Hamburgers were unknown. Dad would have a go at the coconut shy, we all tried the hoopla, I sought to show off at the shooting gallery. We came away with balloons, doomed goldfish in a bowl, and I would try to win a "nice ornament" for Mum, say, a pink china lady in Victorian dress.

The 1953 fair was the last but one we walked up to from Kingston Road. I didn't yet know it but Mum wanted to move from the tall, awkward number 15 and Dad was doing well and we could afford to do so. As we walked home that evening I must have been apprehensive. The next day was the new school, a step into a new milieu, a step that would slowly lead me not away from my family but towards a different sort of life.

Ceremonial portrait 1953.

9
NEW CITIZEN OF A NATION STATE

My new journey to school was on the number three bus, which carried me door to door from almost opposite our house through the centre of the city via Cornmarket and the High, to Iffley Road. I stepped off the bus and crossed the street a little nervous but excited in my new school blazer, black with red piping and the school badge, a lily, on the breast pocket. The motto of Magdalen College School was "Sicut lilium", translated for us as "Like the lily", a little optimistic one might think for a boys' school. The school hymn written by a former head began,

> The lilies bloomed in Galilee,
> Where once the Saviour trod

and concluded,

> God grant us then for Jesus' sake,
> When earthly joys are o'er,
> Our souls in paradise may bloom,
> His lilies evermore.

The music written by an old boy was reminiscent of the tune of "Jerusalem" and soared movingly for paradise blooming before a closing diminuendo for the long-lasting lilies. We sang it proudly, wholeheartedly and with absolutely no sense that the words meant anything to us. "His lilies evermore"? Not, I think, me and my friends. Just words of a hymn. Neither in my early entrancement with the school, nor in later sentimentality about it, could I have stopped to consider the meaning and continued singing without a giggle. We had a school song as well, the march-like "Miles Christi", altogether less soulful. In this we were evidently doing our bit for God rather than asking him to do his bit for us.

That first morning and all following mornings, I wore the school tie, black with thin red diagonal stripe, and on my head the black cap, also with lily badge. I was still in short grey flannel trousers and wore them until the Lower IV form, my third year. Mum and I had bought the uniform, indeed had to buy the uniform, at Hine & Son, "Tailors and Gentlemen's Outfitters", at 52 High Street. The door was set back between two narrow display windows and you entered into a dark, discreet interior to be served by one of the two near identical Hine brothers with their quiet, respectful tones. MCS must have been a very handy monopoly for them. Every couple of years or so boys needed new blazers and caps. For summer, boys could wear a boater rather than a cap. I never came to this, too pretentious, I thought. There were special blazers for senior boys who won full colours for the main sports: black with black piping for rugby, all white for rowing and the very glamourous all scarlet for cricket. Hine & Son also sold suits, tweed sports jackets, cavalry twill trousers, shirts and the like but we only patronised it for school uniform. The premises are now a sweet shop aimed at tourists.

On my shoulders was a brand new leather satchel, for among the many novelties of my new school was homework. I passed through the wide gateway under a line of trees and into what, after Phil and Jim, seemed a vast playground. That same morning, a boy, rather two boys in new brown uniforms, were beginning their careers at City of Oxford High School, boys who might have deserved to be in place of me and my fellow Phil and Jim queue jumper. I never thought about that and, thus, never tried to imagine how different theirs lives might have been without the bent selection. I wonder if Mr Gray's conscience was ever troubled with such thoughts.

Rather, I was seeking to establish new landmarks in the extensive new landscape that lay before me. To my left and parallel to the Iffley Road was a row of black painted wooden buildings, huts in truth. I was to learn that these contained several classrooms, the art room and a small changing room for the first XV. I'm not sure this had any water supply. For the rest of the dayboys I soon learned there was nowhere to change after games save in the classroom. We stuffed sports kit into bag or satchel, put on our clothes and set off sweaty and smelly for the bus home.

In front of me across the concrete playground was a long, solid single-storey block of buildings, pebble dashed and with steeply pitched roofs. This was the hub of the school. In the centre, the largest part of the structure, its gable with clock towards me, was Big School, the place for assemblies, public exams and music or drama performances. Within hung a crude portrait of Cardinal Wolsey, who we were proudly told had been Master at the school, if only for a month. Nearby were honours boards listing those who had won scholarships or exhibitions to Oxford (mainly) and Cambridge.

To the right of Big School the long building contained classrooms and laboratories, later the library; to the left three more classrooms. Separated from it by a narrow gap and at an angle was a large building in the same materials, the chapel. Beyond that, a grassy expanse known as Milham Ford. Nearby were one or two brick and concrete air raid shelters and several other wooden huts. Out of site behind the chapel were two single-storey concrete blocks of classrooms and in the far left hand corner of the site I could glimpse a temporary looking building near the hedge separating the school premises from Christ Church playing field. This was to be my base for the first year.

If I could have then thought in such terms, the whole site was cobbled together on a make do and mend basis. In a few years, a three-storey teaching block including proper changing rooms was added, bringing space, light and showers. A two-storey block of science laboratories followed.

The school served more than 400 boys, sixty or so of whom were boarders. The latter lived out of my ken and that of most dayboys in the nineteenth-century neo-Elizabethan boarding house across Cowley Place. We passed this as we walked or ran to what was the glory of the school in physical terms, the playing field. Over two white-painted, willow pattern bridges we emerged onto a green island, roughly diamond shaped, between two channels of the River Cherwell, an idyllic spot, albeit prone to flooding. Thus, it was often unusable for hockey and rarely offered a firm batting wicket. It was the loveliest field on which to play cricket in summer, overlooked by the pinnacled tower of Magdalen College, the Botanical Gardens and punts making their way alongside Christ Church Meadow from the hire station at Magdalen Bridge. The diving board of the school bathing place was at the far end of the island where the river was deeper. The pretty pavilion was half way along the side overlooked by St Hilda's College. As St Hilda's was an all-female college we grew more interested in overlooking them, than them us. Stories abounded about the female students. Was it true that they bathed naked by moonlight? Some swore they did. We lived in hope of a sighting.

I was joining not just a school but a nation state with its own history, anthems, national heroes, laws, calendar and ceremonials. I was expected to show loyalty, behave patriotically and in time go into battle against our enemies on the sports field. I learned that William Wayneflete, Provost of Eton, Bishop of Winchester and Lord Chancellor of England, had founded the school as part of

Magdalen College around 1480. The pantheon boasted Sir Thomas More as a pupil, Wolsey as a teacher and Captain Noel Chavasse, one of only three men to win the Victoria Cross and bar, as a pupil. Another hallowed former pupil was Sir Basil Blackwell of the booksellers. More hallowed for me were two old boys, Stephen Coles and Bill Lawrence, currently playing scrum half and wing for the Oxford University XV.

This state had its provinces in the form of houses: Chavasse and Leicester was the boarding house, Maltby comprised boys from North Oxford, Walker-Dunn was for Cowley and central city boys, Wilkinson-Blagden for Headington boys and Callender boys from the county.

The laws were explained: you address masters as "Sir" and stand up when one enters the room; school ties to be worn with the option of an open neck white shirt in summer; no running between classes and so on. Masters addressed boys by surnames only and by and large boys did the same with each other. We had not an autumn, spring and summer term as at Phil and Jim but Michaelmas, Hilary and Trinity. Each term we were issued with the school diary, a slim booklet between card covers listing fixtures for the many sports teams, music and drama performances, public examination dates and important visitations. I was excited and a little intimidated that there was so much.

The population of this nation was mixed, though missing both the obviously poor and the demonstrably rich. MCS was a direct grant school with about half the boys fee-paying and half on free places funded by either the state or the local authority. Its main visible link with Magdalen College was the young choristers who all wore grey flannel suits. Each morning they marched in twos over Magdalen Bridge in academic gowns and mortar boards to rehearse in the college chapel, returning there for evensong after school. Out of my sight, the college was heavily represented on the governing body and owned the land on which the school was built. I don't recall entering the college buildings until I went to a school performance of the St John Passion when I was seventeen. It was later emphasised that attending the school was no aid to being admitted to the college.

Yet by becoming a citizen of this state I was, without considering it, taking a step on the bridge from town to gown. To me the name of the school had just been a name. It began to dawn - with the sight of the choristers, the lily badge taken from the college shield, the college tower standing watch over the playing field - that my new life was no longer separate from the university.

A number of boys were the offspring of college fellows and university professors, some of them famous academics, not that I knew. Nikolaas Tinbergen and Dorothy Hodgkin, both to be Nobel Laureates, had boys there, as did the historian A.J.P. Taylor; Dylan Thomas' son, Llewelyn, was a boarder. The parents of my first friends were all town people: a bank manager, greengrocer, accountant at Morris Motors, manager at Elliston's and owner of a printing business. At the age of thirteen there came a small influx of boys from Oxford prep schools, Dragon School and New College School. Among them were more sons of distinguished academics.

For the first years, we had lessons mainly in our form rooms, the masters coming to us. The signal for the end of a lesson was, as it been for centuries, a boy ringing a hand bell in the playground where it could be heard throughout the school. An electric bell was finally installed in 1957. The rhythm of my life was changed by homework which was set for every evening. As we had lessons on Saturday mornings a sixth lot of homework was set for the weekend. We had many tests and our written work was assiduously marked. Every two weeks came the "fortnightly order" by which boys were listed from top to bottom in each class according to their marks. This was read out in class and the top names in school assembly. We were given our individual position paper to take home to parents. No hiding.

The day began with the register marked off by hand in black (present) or red (absent) ink. Then we attended chapel. The chaplain conducted affairs, a prefect read the lesson and occasionally there was a bit of extra entertainment when a boy would throw up, seeking to escape to the toilets but getting only so far as the aisle. No avoiding a prayer or two, of course, and we always sang a hymn, the best bit for me, especially when it was one of the great Anglican chartbusters: "For All the Saints", "Dear Lord and Father of Mankind", "Guide me O Thou Great Redeemer", "Love Divine All Love Excelling". We never sang what apparently passes for a hymn today, "Morning Has Broken", not then turned into a pop song by Cat Stevens, nor would the school have countenanced John Lennon's soppy anthem, "Imagine", even if it had been written. On the last day of term, we had "God Be with You Till We Meet Again", which in later years could make me well up, even though I would see my chums the following day.

> Keep love's banner floating o'er you,
> Smite death's threat'ning wave before you,
> God be with you till we meet again.

Chapel was often a time for important announcements. The worst I recall was one Monday when a boy called Tony Kane had been killed in a car accident over the weekend. He was a popular and good looking boy, an outstanding hockey player, and there was genuine grief. My main memory, however, is the end of the service as one of his team mates walked slowly and dramatically down the aisle, he was very sad I knew but he was also performing very sad.

The ruler of this small state was Bob Stanier, who gave a tearful address when Kane died. He had held the post of Master for nine years when I arrived. The friendly and liberal atmosphere of the school was a reflection of his personality. He was below average height with a broad nose, crinkly, grey hair and spectacles. He stood with head tilted slightly back, his gaze measuring one and lips pressed as if waiting to speak. When he did so, it was in a careful, precise manner which compelled attention. He had a powerful and calming presence, slightly distant and never chummy. The overall sense was of a firm but benign wizard holding sway. He was polite and courteous to all, particularly welcoming to Mum and Dad as they became regular attendees at school events. In supporting me, and later David, they were stepping up into a new world; I suspect the kindly Bob recognised this.

In Bob Stanier's life as in his school there was room for many expressions of human fulfilment. He had played rugby for the university Greyhounds, he played golf and cricket, at which he was quite the slowest of leg break bowlers tossing the ball up in a high tempting arc. He painted watercolours, played double bass in the school orchestra, was an expert on heraldry and had written a history of the school. He learned Russian so he could read *War and Peace* in the original. His grasp of the language did not extend to speaking it and when a Soviet woman educationalist came to the school, all he could offer in her language was the first lines of a Pushkin poem, which translated as

I loved you: yet the love, maybe,
Has not extinguished in my heart.

The occasion, it seems, never recovered. Bob wrote with a beautiful italic script and he encouraged us to do the same. One or two boys succeeded in mastering the sloping nib and still wrote quickly enough to complete essays on time. I set forth on the italic journey but arrived only at an ugly hybrid hand.

He and his wife, Maida, had taken in a Jewish refugee before the war, taught him English and found him a job; in 1956 after the Soviet invasion they adopted a Hungarian refugee. When a former schoolmate of his was charged with being a male prostitute, Bob appeared as a witness in his defence and when the man was given five years in gaol, wrote frequently to him. Bob was chair of Oxford Marriage Guidance Council and a campaigner on traffic matters, proposing, to the scorn of the council, something very much like park and ride ten years before the council introduced it. His greatest prominence in the city was as chair of Oxford Campaign for Nuclear Disarmament, about which he was passionate, even a little dotty. He always wore the badge in his buttonhole, to the discomfort of some boys and parents and, as I later discovered, to the amazement of other heads at the Headmasters' Conference.

He was liberal in nearly all matters but a school had to have rules and they needed to be enforced. Chapel was compulsory unless the boy was Catholic or Jewish. Bob justified this when questioned, "Life is a battle if we want to make the world a better place. We cannot afford to be too choosey about our allies. As the officer in command I have to plan the campaign. Christianity is a force for the good and chapel is its voice." Corporal punishment was part of the law enforcement apparatus. The ultimate sanction was for Bob to beat a boy. This was rare and I knew of no instance of it. No other masters beat. The school police were the prefects, who dished out lines ("Write, 'I must not throw rubbish, 100 times'") and for some offences could beat a boy on the bottom with a special, crook handle bamboo cane. They hurt, and remain available, though not for use in schools. (When I googled "school cane" I was offered one for £6.99p - from "UberKinky.co.uk".) I was beaten twice, three strokes in my second term for walking on Milham Ford when it had been declared out of bounds, and later for cheeking a prefect by answering him with my hands in my pockets. I did not like this practice.

Bob showed another limit to his liberalism. The arrangement for prize-winners was that the boy went to Parker's bookshop, selected a book of suitable value and gave his name. The books were sent to the Master who stuck in the school prize plate and in his elegant italic hand wrote the boy's name and the subject in which he had excelled. The book was then presented at the prize-giving by the invited dignitary. When Richard Warnock selected a prize in the sixth form, he was summoned by Bob ahead of the ceremony and handed the book in his study. It was a publication of some notoriety, *The Shook-Up Generation*, an account of juvenile delinquency in the United States by Harrison Salisbury. Among the activities it described was the circle jerk, of which no more here. Bob explained that while Richard should have the book of his choice, this was not one that should carry the imprimatur of the school at a formal school event. When Richard looked inside he saw the MCS plate had indeed been stuck in before being torn out. Bob must have inscribed it before discovering the contents.

Bob did some teaching. After two years, the top set for Latin had no choice but to drop geography to learn Greek, taught by him. To my, and I'm sure his, irritation I was among this group, coming bottom in a class for the only time. It wasn't just my Greek that upset him. "He would do better if he did not 'loll' so much," he wrote on my report.

My class in the first year was 2a, the new intake from the eleven plus exam, boys from both the city and county. It shared a shack-like building with 2b, the previous year's first form. Each classroom was heated by a huge solid fuel stove which stood near the master's desk. In 2b naughtier boys peed on it to create a dreadful stench. 2b were the old hands and advertised their know-how, monopolising the pile of sand that constituted a downhill racetrack for Dinky racing cars. In the previous year their form master, Mr Arnold-Craft, "Crafty Arnold", had conducted, or rather had them conduct, a form court to deal with breaches of the rules. They implied that the sophistication of all this was something we newcomers could barely conceive. In 2a it was the time of sizing each other up, who were rivals in sport or in lessons, whom did we like, who lived near in case the great leap to meeting outside school might be made.

My form master was Horace Elam, known as "Wettoe". He was just right for us new boys, a kindly man who once told a colleague that his definition of an honest boy was one who did not look you straight in the eye when telling a lie. Wettoe had curly hair and a big, soft face on a strong neck. A gap separated his two front teeth and his usual expression was a slightly goofy but utterly good natured grin. He enjoyed pretending to be shocked. "Boy!" he would cry at a silly answer or memory lapse, and lean forward with raised eyebrow and can-you-believe-it grin as if he'd heard the vicar say "bloody". Masters wore black academic gowns when teaching and Wettoe would clutch the ends of his and wrap them around himself in excitement or for emphasis. He taught maths, set the school general knowledge paper, directed or co-directed the annual

Shakespeare production and ran the school camp to which he drove in his snazzy motor, a pale green Triumph convertible. Wettoe was housemaster for the boarding house. He had been at the school since the beginning of the forties and was to retire there. I heard that he had once nearly become engaged but his partner at MCS was his black Labrador, Patricia. As maths teacher Wettoe helped me to a good start at Magdalen. I was regularly at or near the top of the fortnightly orders and at the end of the first year won two of the four class prizes, for maths and French, flattering to deceive in the long term as it turned out.

The French master under whom I did so well was "Tich" Symonds. Short, straight backed and sharply dressed, he exuded a crisp authority. We rose to our feet as he swept into the classroom and assumed immediate command: "Dépêchez-vous", then "Taisez-vous." I thought he was terrific. He took mass physical jerks standing on the roof of an air raid shelter with a megaphone. Then one day he was suddenly not there. Was it something to do with the sea scouts which he led? Or the trip to France with some of the boys? In so much as we thought about it at the time, which was not very, the general opinion was it was something fishy. I was later to learn more. Symonds had asked Anderson, one of the dayboys in my year, if he had ever risen early on May Morning to hear the college choir sing a Latin hymn from the top of Magdalen tower.

"There is always a crowd as it's a great Oxford event and something to experience." Anderson hadn't been to this.

"Would you like to?" asked Symonds. Anderson said he would. As he lived just outside Oxford, it was arranged with his parents that rather than travel into Oxford by five thirty in the morning, the boy would stay overnight at Symonds' house near the school. At bedtime, Anderson climbed into the double bed he was assigned.

Soon after, Symonds came into the room and groomed himself elaborately before slipping into the same bed. When it was evident that this was not welcome, Symonds asked, "Would you rather I make up another bed for you?"

"Yes, Sir."

He did so. There was another boy staying over for whom, Anderson sensed, such things may have been perfectly agreeable but he could not be sure. Next day, he rang his mother from school. She came and took her son to see Bob Stanier who listened to the story.

"Anderson," he asked, "would you be happy still being taught by Mr Symonds?" There was a pause before the boy replied.

"No, Sir."

Symonds left the school. We heard that he went to a smart boys' school in the United States.

Another disappearance in similar circumstances was when a senior boarder in our year was reported to have left the school over the weekend. What had happened, we wanted to know? The word from the boarding house was that he had been caught kissing the gangly Shortclffe, a chorister, on the stairs. Several decades later I met the older boy when our paths crossed professionally. We had a pleasant lunch with no mention of the above story although within a minute or so of sitting down he eagerly told me about both a first wife and a second. Just in case.

In that first year, I soon lost myself in the school and quickly identified with everything MCS. I watched the first XV in home matches, I went to the school play, *Hamlet*, starring Martin Bowley, later QC, and Mum, Dad and I attended all three parts of Commemoration, the big event of the year in early July. First came the Commem service in St Mary the Virgin, the university church, then the school prize-giving in the Town Hall and in the afternoon the cricket and tennis matches against the old boys on School Field. For the last, the dress code for boys was school blazer, open neck white shirt and cricket flannels. When we arrived back at Kingston Road I remained in this rig rather longer than was necessary so I could swank along to the newsagents making sure I was seen.

The chief school sports were rugby in the autumn, hockey in the spring and cricket in summer. The new boys who hadn't played rugby before were put in a group and asked questions about the rules. I was quick to answer as I had picked them up from televised games until I deliberately got one wrong so as not to show off.

"When the ball is put in the scrum what happens?"

"The hooker tries to win it for his side."

"How does he do this?"

"With his hand."

"No, Wyatt. He uses his foot."

As I well knew.

I wasn't very big but enjoyed rugby and in the second year was in the school Under 13 team. On a murky November afternoon, we played Dragon School, whom we feared, on their ground. I was in the front row and after about fifteen minutes was in some pain from my left shoulder. I told the ref and went off to see the master in charge, Mr Swann, on the touchline.

"Where does it hurt?"

"In my shoulder, Sir"

"Well, Wyatt, I suppose you can come off the field if you really want to."

After that, I had to play on and did so. That evening I sat cradling my aching arm. My parents and I thought it would improve but after a nearly week it had not and Mum took me to the doctor. He took one look and said, "You have broken you collar bone," adding, "We'll put your arm in a sling and it will mend, nothing else to be done." It did mend. But they had let me play on. Today would we sue?

My early friends were made among the sporty: Alan Pemberton, "Pem", a short, powerfully built boy who had been born in Birmingham and could affect a near impenetrable Brummie accent. Richard Warnock, "Nock", the well-spoken son of a bank manager, was a natural ball player. Robert Herbertson, "Sherb", tall, red faced and red haired, slightly clumsy, became the school's star athlete. Terry Collier was tall, dark haired and good looking, flashy at everything he did and dubbed, possibly by himself, "Tex". Clive Oliver, "Olly", with a flopping mop of almost white hair, was a good tennis player. His father, a local Football Association official, took Olly and me to see England beat Scotland 7-2 at Wembley in 1955. John Martin arrived from New College School at thirteen and immediately joined our group. Tall, fresh faced, with tight curly hair, outstanding at cricket and hockey, he also had a single figure golf handicap.

We argued over teams we supported and debated international selections. We watched what sport there was on television and when, in April 1954, the BBC began a regular Wednesday evening programme, Sportsview, Pem was utterly convinced he was responsible as he had written to the BBC two weeks earlier suggesting just such a show. The following month Roger Bannister ran the first four-minute mile just a few hundred yards up the Iffley Road from the school.

We played football in the playground in breaks and after lunch. The school had no canteen but an arrangement with the municipal restaurant just off St Clement's, near where the Florey Building is now. Boys trooped across three roads to get there with no casualties as far as I know. The "Muni" was a self-service restaurant run by the local council, a hangover from the British Restaurants opened during the Second World War to provide cheap, nourishing food. We bought "dinner tickets" which we redeemed for cottage pie, fish and chips, cauliflower cheese and the like. It was not always up to scratch and Pem once caused a memorable ruckus complaining about an undercooked sausage.

"Look, it's pink inside."

"It's meant to be that colour."

"No sausage should look like that. Where is the manager?"

"The manager's not coming just to see you…"

From the third form, my second year, we were grouped alphabetically for most subjects with sets for maths, French and Latin. Tim Mendham was in my form. He would pull back his sleeve to announce with a straight face, "By the hairs on my wrist I make it ten past twelve of the clock." Tim developed into a fast bowler and fielded with a prodigious throw, reaching the stumps from the longest of boundaries. Ken Hunt distinguished himself by his huge, echoing burps, "Grandfathers", as they were known. He would stand at one end of the grassy Milham Ford as friends listened at the other end, seventy yards away, to see if the sound carried.

Two clever, naughty brothers would gang up, running around an Anglo-Indian boy shouting "Pakistani! Pakistani!" Now and then an excited chant of "In a bate, in a bate" signalled that a victim was being picked on. Spectacles were a common factor among the tormented. A clever, gentle boy called "Bruno" Horncastle was one such. He was a kind and friendly ambassador to the new boys in my first months, pushing his round specs back up his nose with fingers stretched wide and a surprised look. The bespectacled Wiggins was the worst bullied, with few friends, an easy target as victims usually are. He was always head down in a book. Dornford Yates was a favourite, as he shuffled, pigeon toed, around the school. I remember him in tears. Why didn't I intervene?

Perhaps I did. I hope so.

In the garden at 51 Sunderland Avenue, soon after moving, with our dog Chris.

10
MOVING ON AND UP

n the meantime, we moved house. Mum found the four floors of Kingston Road hard work. She and Dad looked for somewhere new and found a semi-detached house in Templar Road, Cutteslowe. They took David and me to see it and resolved to go to the estate agents the following day to sign the contract. That very evening Mum's brother, Walter, by now a big developer in the city, rang to say that a plot of land in Sunderland Avenue, where he lived on the northern edge of the city, was about to come on the market. Did Dad want it? He must decide quickly as once it was advertised for sale many would be many after it.

Dad was a bricklayer and builder. Here was an opportunity to build his own house for the family. He said he would buy. As luck would have it, the woman who was renting Mum and Dad's house on the Eynsham Road had just moved, so they sold that, paid off the mortgage and bought the plot at 51 Sunderland Avenue on the south, city, side of the road. Dad remembered the price as about £700. Most but not all plots on this side of the road had been built on in the past twenty years with an eclectic mix of good sized detached houses. They had a short drive and some planting in front, a large garden to the rear. It was an aspirational road for the commercial middle classes

This was an exciting time for the whole of our aspirational family. Dad did the brickwork, the tiling and much else himself. As the house neared completion, we spent time there at the weekend, Dad working, the rest of us planning what would go where, enjoying the smells of sawn timber and fresh paint that were leading us to a new life. The house was set back a little on the plot behind a low brick wall, a small front garden and a not quite drive. It was a detached, two-storey, double fronted house with, to the left of the front door, unusual flat fronted bay windows, to the right windows flush with the wall. At ground level there was a skirt of red brick which became the front door surround, the rest of the walls pebble dashed. To the left was a garage. It looked a comfortable, friendly house and my parents were flattered when soon after we moved in two passing cars stopped to ask how they could have a similar home.

Sunderland Avenue was actually on the A40 ring road but set back behind a wide verge and a service road, so it was much less noisy than one might expect. The bay window room on the ground floor was the dining room, in effect our living room, for the table was mostly pushed against the wall and in the corner sat the KB television. We ate here at Christmas or on a big family occasion, food passing through what I thought the ultimate in modern living, a hatch. The large kitchen itself was part tiled in green, the surfaces and table top covered in a green, tweedy patterned Formica, the product of the day. The narrow basement kitchen at Kingston Road had a cramped outlook to a small brick-lined area and limited sky; now Mum looked out from the sink onto a wide view of our garden and the trees in others. A glass door opened from the kitchen to the garden; on the other side was the back entrance of the house. Outside here was a storage shed and bunkers for coal and for the coke with which Dad stoked up the central heating boiler every morning. A door led to the rear of the garage where Dad constructed a small office where he could do his "booking".

The front door of the house was oak, also the frame of the staircase which was filled with two frosted glass panels. Across the hall from the dining room was the through lounge, a window to the road to the front and a French window, later a glassed-in loggia, to the garden. Mum went to town in here, decorating in what I came to realise was a busy fashion, with a new three-piece suite upholstered in dark red patterned fabric, standing on a patterned pink carpet surrounded by flowery wall paper. It was a statement that said, I have nice things now. My first record player was kept in the lounge where I could play what Dad called "that bloody honky tonk stuff" out of his hearing. Upstairs were three bedrooms, parents' above the lounge, David's at the front over the dining room and mine to the rear overlooking the garden. I was allowed to choose the colour of paint here, eau de nil. It was a show off choice. I was trying to impress myself. The one bathroom was off the landing, fittings and tiles selected by Mum, in pink and grey.

The garden was mostly grass, which served for cricket and football, in both of which I could display my superior skills to my five-year younger brother. Dad would bowl at us sometimes and at others revisit his football triumphs with East Oxford Corinthians by demonstrating "the low drive". The second year we were there I ruined a Sunday by kicking a rugby ball in the air and diving to catch it, breaking the collar bone I had not broken before. I stumbled into the house in a streaming cold sweat just as lunch was to be served and Dad had to drive me to the Radcliffe Infirmary and a four-hour wait. The plot to the east of ours was left vacant for a few years. On the other side, David and I had ball trouble, for balls do go over fences and into next door gardens. This was irritating for our neighbours but should not have been as irritating as they made it appear. When they threw the football back there was no real need to burst it first. Family relations with Mr and Mrs Riddell were never good. They were an unsmiling Scottish couple, he I think the city engineer. I expect that he ensured that Oxford's infrastructure was well ordered but he and his wife turned a stern, unfriendly face to us. We suspected we were not the right kind of neighbours. They'd been hoping for something better. At the bottom of the garden

Dad began to cultivate a vegetable garden. He exulted in young sweet carrots, new potatoes, fresh peas, runner and broad beans. Mum had roses, pink naturally, in the front.

The unspoken thought was that we had moved up one. The road was named Sunderland after the Earldom of Sunderland, one of the titles accumulated by the Duke of Marlborough, the former landowner. "51 Sunderland", we thought, had a ring. Dad bought a newer and slightly larger car, a black Morris Oxford. We must have had a telephone before this but I only remember our new solid black apparatus answering to Oxford 57727. It rested just inside the front door on a special oak double shelf, phone on top, directory below. Telephone lines were provided by a state monopoly and were not automatically available. We asked each other at school, "Are you on the phone?" In other words, do you have one? Our case for getting a line was Dad's business need. Even so, we had a shared line at first until Dad complained that he could not have a confidential conversation about his work if the party line users could pick up their receiver and listen in. I was allowed to use the phone, not that I conducted anything resembling a conversation on it for many years. Calls were abbreviated.

"Nock, is the Thomas Cromwell essay for tomorrow?... Oh, good. Cheers."

Or "Hello John... OK, we'll meet at the Cadena. Bye."

Or perhaps if feeling voluble, "Pem? It's Will. Are you going to the Headington match? Who else is coming?... I'll cycle with you."

All my friends called me Will, to Mum's understandable irritation. She attempted a reargued action when answering the phone. "I don't know a Will. Would you like to speak to Alan?"

In the more spacious and easier to run house the pressure on Mum was lifted. We had central heating, a washing machine and

Dad liked to help with the cooking at weekends. Sundays was always a roast. "Don't we live to what the poor do?" he liked to ask before urging, "Let battle commence" and tucking in. If there were two kinds of food his question was, "Suety or plain?" I remember the bacon and onion clanger, a suet pudding, from Kingston Road, but I don't associate it or a spotted dick with our new improved status. That could be my mind shuffling memories into their proper place. Mum cooked our weekday evening meal for when we came in from school. If we were late for any reason it would, like Dad's, be dished up onto a plate, covered with a saucepan lid or second plate and put into the oven to keep warm. When retrieved, the edge of the plate carried a sticky brown decoration, where gravy had leaked under the saucepan lid. It was a carnivorous household. Monday was usually curried beef or lamb from the remains of the roast, Tuesday, often lamb chops, Wednesday stew and dumplings and Thursday perhaps pork chops. Friday nearly always fried fish.

Sometimes I had need of a snack. Scrambled egg sandwiches with grated cheese satisfied this after sport on Saturday afternoons, sardines on toast at other times. A lettuce and sugar sandwich had its moments, as did the lettuce and crisp sandwich, the cold potato, tomato and salad cream sandwich and the spam and tomato sandwich. Fried spam was more of a meal. Spaghetti and ravioli came only in tins. Aubergines, peppers, courgettes and garlic all lay in the future. The only restaurant I can recall going to was a Lyons Corner House on a family trip to London. I was tremendously impressed by the sophistication of my cousin Mary's husband, Jim Campbell, when he ordered the Nanking Special. I was further impressed when the, no doubt pseudo, Chinese compilation arrived and he ate it. Jim had been a steward on ocean liners. Dad liked plain cooking and was wary of any, what he dubbed, "noshy up sort of a business".

On a summer Sunday we would usually go for "a ride round"; in winter we had what Mum called a beano, sitting round a small table in the lounge with chocolate and sweets and playing Monopoly or its horse racing partner, Totopoly, possible rummy. We had a good quality, well-balanced roulette wheel, mostly kept for a larger group at Christmas. We all liked a bet. David and I drank lemonade, orangeade or cream soda, large bottles of which along with squash were delivered weekly to our door by the Corona man. Dad had a bottle of beer, Mum a Scotch. I don't think I ever saw either of them drink too much. Dad was a two pint man at most and didn't have much time for anyone who was "half cut". At Christmas in later years Mum might look a bit bright-eyed and say she felt a bit "drunky".

Mum was quite small, or "petite" as she would rather have it, and found David and me trying at times: two sporty boys charging about the house and garden, eating enormous amounts of food, shouting, laughing, teasing her and in my case beginning to show signs of considering himself superior. "Don't mommer me," was her cry when I was holding forth or asking questions or, "It flummoxes me." Sometimes she had had enough, said, "You're a right little devil," and went to the broom cupboard to retrieve her "little squitchy stick", a feather duster on a length of bamboo. She would chase me round the kitchen trying to land a whack, even when I was seventeen. She was both angry and finding it funny at the same time; I laughed but knew I had gone too far.

Dave and I told her often enough, as children do, that she was the "best mum in the world", and the "best cook in the world", and meant it although I fear the latter was not true. For her there was a right way of doing things that she had learned and we should learn them too. What "the gentry" did was her yardstick. While she never put it baldly, it mattered to her what people thought of you.

I was much influenced in this. Even now, I have to correct spelling, punctuation and grammar in an email as if it were a letter. Why? I guess I don't want to risk people thinking I don't know better. I need to demonstrate that I am at ease with what doesn't come naturally. I picked up that my betters asked, "How do you do?" when introduced, not expecting an answer, rather than claiming, "Pleased to meet you." I noted that it was an affectation to tip the soup dish away rather than towards one. My eye and ear for such things probably grew to be more sensitive than Mum's but the impulse was the same.

She was never entirely easy with her favourite brother, Walter's, new family. He and his wife Aggie had "parted birds' eggs", as Dad put it. Aggie would never divorce him but he had set up home with a lively Welsh redhead with the same name as Mum, Hettie. "Mrs H", as we called her, overflowed with screeching talk, laughter and mad ideas. She conducted life noisily, good heartedly and eccentrically, keeping her own small pet rescue in her garden, rabbits and Paddy the seagull shipped by train from Cornwall, among the saved until taken by a fox. She took tea most days at the Randolph Hotel, whither a daughter caught the bus after school to join her and do her homework. Now, we were just a couple of hundred yards along the road from where she lived with Walter and their three pretty girls in a huge house on a double plot. My parents who were both prone to ask, "what do you think of this carrying on then?" when the sixties arrived, had to make peace with the carrying on in the family. Walter had always looked after Mum, it was through him we had our new home, and once or twice a year we would visit or receive them as two families. Walter, a man of few words, had a touch of charisma. He took Dad, David and me to see his racehorses, gave us a ride in his Rolls and took us into his study to see his own private ticker tape machine, by which he took swiftest delivery of the racing results - this last I'd seen only in films.

Walter provided for the two children of his marriage to Aggie and built new houses for them next door to each other in Cornwallis Road at the foot of Iffley Hill. His son Denis went into his father's business and eventually ran it. He was a big, clumsy fellow, fair of hair and skin, with a Hooper's moon face and an expression of perpetual mischief. He charged into a room throwing out a challenge or comic insult. He and his dark haired Scottish wife, Janet, and small son and daughter were close to our family, sharing noisy, laughing visits over Christmas or Easter and joining holidays. We saw his sister Mary and her Scottish husband Jim less often. Mary was a lovely, warm and gentle person. Their first daughter Judith was born with a hole in the heart or similar and had restrictive growth. I would occasionally catch a bus to go to play with her, not wholly unaware of "how kind" I was being. Jim got on Dad's nerves in that he was always boasting or telling improbable stories in a "show offy" way, anathema to Mum and Dad. He would do this, he would do that, he had a plan for something else. I know that Walter set him up in at least one business, a Scottish restaurant, which failed. Dad implied there were others. Mrs H meanwhile provided a regular source of can-you-believe-it stories for Mum, who liked her, could laugh with as well as at her, but was always on edge about the irregularity of her presence.

These were busy years for Dad as he took on bigger jobs. It was a boom time for council building and he won contracts for new bungalows, houses and flats in Oxfordshire and Berkshire, as well alterations to others and building some private houses. He took on more men though it was difficult to find enough good labour. He used to complain wearily that the larger firms had the pick of the better tradesmen and labourers; he had to make do with the remainder. A rock from the mid-1950s till his retirement was Joe Todorovic, a Yugoslavian known as "Joe the Pole", Poland being where most men with funny names came from at that time. He could not return to Yugoslavia, I was told, because he had been a supporter of King Peter and the country was governed by Marshal Tito's Communist regime. Joe's English was a bit strangled but he always had a smile for David and me, slipping an uncalled for half a crown, insisting we keep it. I think Dad was enormously fond of him.

We would hear his exasperation with some of the other men: "he is a bloody closet," or "he hadn't a clue, he was running about like a lamplighter." Dad spent sixty years on building sites but I never heard him use any stronger swear word than "bloody". There were tales of Brucicer, one of the "Bagarses" from Leafield, and "Eynsham Harry", who came from Long Hanborough and shared his girlfriend with the dustman. Harry's mother rang the site one day to say that he shouldn't drink his tea because she realised she had made it in a Durazone weed killer bottle. It was too late, he had already drunk it. Another Harold bemoaned his wife buying a Hoover from the door to door salesman to clean the carpets of which they had none. Walt Murray, "a hermit sort of a fellow", according to Dad, liked to do a little tap dance on the scaffolding. He lived in a primitive brick shack he had built himself but disliked the sound of the wind whistling through the telegraph wires on the pole outside. So he chopped the telegraph pole down. A labourer who lodged at a village store thought he would do his landlords a favour when they went out for the day by letting the pig out of the sty to eat the weeds in their garden. He neglected to tell the pig to leave the vegetables alone. Reflecting on this time, Dad said "You can tell the sort I had."

Some of the men went straight to the work site for the 7.30 start, others came to the house by 7.10 and were driven by Dad. He enjoyed the site work but became very tired and worried when he had to juggle two jobs, act as foreman bricklayer and then do the office work in the evenings. Ted Skuse still helped with the estimates but Dad had to go through each one. Dad wrote out all his business letters by hand and a friend called Harry Wordman, who worked in the office at Elliston's, came a couple of evenings a week to type them. Harry was a gentlemanly fellow whose wife got on well with Mum, so the four would go for a drink together at weekends. A new figure, Mr Dawson the accountant, stepped into our lives, when in 1956, with sixteen council houses at Great Haseley under way, Dad turned his business into a company. His hopes were evident in its name, Basil Wyatt and Sons. Whether he ever thought both of us would go into the business I never knew, but in one regard his hope was realised: David took it over, expanded it greatly and runs it still. In my late teens, I did odd errands for Dad, and when a brick lorry chose to deliver on a Saturday, David and I put on canvas gloves and unloaded at the site.

Mum's role, which she loved, was as cashier. She caught the bus into town to draw out cash for the payroll from the Westminster Bank in the High. She liked holding the money and continued to collect the substantial sums required until well into her seventies. Once when she was unable to go and Dad went himself, the bank staff debated before they would let him pick up the money usually collected by Mrs Wyatt. Mum worked out the wages, entered the sums in the costs book, counted out the correct sums and filled the pay packets. Dad would sometimes watch her through a window enjoying the pleasure she took in handling the readies. She was ever one for salting away a little money and having a secret cache.

Twenty or more years later, searching for something in an upstairs cupboard Dad found books of her five shilling savings stamps going back to the early years of their marriage. Mum had forgotten about them. The saving was the fun. I think it gave her some control over the future. Also, she was secretive, possibly of what she considered family shame, more likely it was her nature. In years to come she would buy the latest colour in the cardigans she liked from Elliston's and put it away, so that when she eventually wore it she could truthfully answer the question, "Is that new?" with "No, I bought it ages ago." When she died at 83, there were two complete Jaeger outfits unworn in her wardrobe.

These were years when they began to move out into the world more. They had always enjoyed going for a drink, to the cinema and on holiday. Now Mum joined the Wolvercote Women's' Institute and the school's parents' association, helping at the Christmas Fair and with teas. Being in with the crowd was not their natural environment but confidence was growing. I believe they felt that being visible around the school was how they gave their sons a bunk up. Mum was the more adventurous. She liked to dress up and always had a good sense of what suited her, neither under or overdressing for her age. When a press ball was advertised in Oxford Mum was keen to go, thinking she might meet again people she knew when working in Twining's Wine Lounge. Unknown to any of us she went by bus to Sandford on Thames to borrow an evening gown from a friend. Came the day, I arrived home from school to find Mum upset. Dad didn't want to go. He thought it all might be a bit too posh for him. I hated seeing Mum disappointed and said I would cycle back into town to hire Dad a dinner jacket and bow tie if he would go. He agreed and off I dashed to Walters in The Turl. He had no black shoes, so blacked over a brown pair while I was gone. They went to the ball and to others later.

Just a few streets away was my mother's sister Ginny, living in a sheltered home after release from Littlemore Hospital. David and I knew nothing of this. My parents visited her but never revealed her existence, just as Mum concealed the disorderly shape of her family. Perhaps it was a matter of why drag it all up now? Difficult to broach the subject. Or was there, too, an irrational fear that if it all came out, then the improvements in her life over the years, the steps up she had taken, the hard won position in the world might crumble? That your origins chained you to the past and progression was ever threatened by an escaped secret?

As my parents stepped out into Oxford. I had no clear idea of what I would do and where I would do it. As a small boy, I liked the idea of being a lawyer, it sounded important. In early teens, I thought of the army, again important and a uniform to swank in. These were both passing caprices. In reality I hadn't begun to engage with the thought of a grown-up job. I do think that, without articulating the thought, I did not expect to remain in Oxford all my life. Subconsciously, I saw life as a progression, moving on to the next thing, moving up the while. That's how school was structured, after all. Following this would likely be university, then work, then marriage. The sharpened pencil of the eleven plus day prodded me forward and would keep prodding.

RAF Laarbruch. Far left:
J.S."Sid" Millward, next to
him Peter Arnold-Craft. Far
right WW.

11
"FILM STARS. I SEE. MMM..."

Recently, an artist friend, Allen Jones, told me how he had failed the eleven plus but that after a year his parents received a letter saying a terrible mistake had been made. There was now a place for him at Ealing Grammar School. The Jones family discovered that a local shopkeeper had bribed the primary school head with groceries so that his son would go to Ealing Grammar. The story came to light when the boy failed to keep up academically and had been removed from the school. Had that primary head been up to Mr Gray's chicanery? Was it malpractice that swept the shopkeeper's son through the eleven plus? Hard to see how it could have been otherwise. For Allen Jones, the wrong had been righted. Was there a boy, or boys, at City of Oxford High School whose parents should have received such a letter saying their son should be at Magdalen instead of my Phil and Jim chum and me? But I was keeping up.

After a year, I was at home at MCS, after two years it was part of my identity. By walking 100 yards from our new house to the Woodstock Road roundabout I could still catch a bus, the number four, direct to school. I often shared the journey home with the shy, likeable Robin Pye, younger of the two Pye brothers. The Pye family were Oxford's most prominent developers and they lived in a huge early twentieth-century house on the corner of Woodstock Road and Squitchey Lane. Mrs Pye was the great panjandrum of the parents' association and the family's charitable trust supported many good causes in the city, particularly musical activities. Robin played the flute. He was a tightly wound up boy, his voice almost caricature posh and was hard to get to know. Many years later I was told he had a breakdown and was arrested trying to hold up an American air base with a cutlass and twelve bore shotgun.

Soon I was cycling to school, first on a standard black bicycle before progressing to a dark red, drop handlebar racing bike with derailleur gears. The derailleurs signalled coolness and were to bikes what GTi would be to small cars twenty years hence. The racing bike was not only faster and more stylish, it allowed for a greater variety of poses both in motion and at rest. A black saddle bag was augmented by two panier bags either side of the rear wheels to transport increasing quantities of books, notes and sports gear.

My route was a scenic one, along the leafy Banbury Road through Summertown and passing three girls' schools: the gate to Greycotes, the turn off to Oxford High School, where goddesses lurked, and the buildings of Wychwood, a boarding and thus less interesting establishment. From Parks Road I sometimes cut through the university science laboratories, sometimes rode on and along Holywell to Longwall Street. Left into The High, over Magdalen Bridge to the Plain, and into the cul de sac, Cowley Place, leading to the school main gate. It made for an exhilarating ride on a fine morning and had its pleasures even when enveloped in a yellow oilskin cape and sou'wester in the rain. In retrospect, what a privilege for that to be my daily journey.

By now, school friendships were well established and the bike made meeting up outside school easier, although in term there was little time for it. I never went out on a weekday evening as I had "prep". If the weather caused midweek games to be cancelled I might go to the pictures with a friend that afternoon. We had something new to study in films. A friend of Pem's brother had it on good authority that when film stars kissed they avoided lips touching lips, placing them just to the side of or below the mouth, so the man would not get an erection - we were all too aware of how easily that could happen. Our observations concluded that the stars often came pretty damned close to lip on lip action but there was no hint as to what was happening down below. We were decades away from the great tongue swallowing gob smackers that were to come.

If Saturday afternoon was free of a match, then we were off to watch football. We played scratch games of soccer in the holidays and, in summer, tennis. I liked to go to the Pitt Rivers Museum in Parks Road. This was a treasure trove of archaeological and ethnographic exhibits from all over the world. The high point of a visit was marvelling at the shrunken heads from the upper Amazon, reading how the enemy's head had been skinned, brain and skull discarded, then filled with hot sand and moulded into shape. The little dark faces, lips and eyes sown up, were crowded together in their endless sleep. A great mystery, never then solved, was what the little knives labelled "Female circumcision" were for. We knew well enough what circumcision was, but what on earth was there to cut from a front bottom? Twenty-five years later I discovered when helping to the television screen a graphic documentary about female genital mutilation in Africa.

We explored the Ashmolean. The great treasure here was said to be the Anglo-Saxon Alfred Jewel, so I regularly went to take a look, anti-climax that it was. More fun was searching the collection of Greek vases to find the rude ones on which men had funny, pointy cocks. Best of all was the large dusty room of old master paintings where my favourite was Uccello's *The Hunt in the Forest*. The stylised horses and riders and prancing hounds are chasing deer which race this way and that among the trees, the whole an appealing, energetic and well-ordered design. With homework and regular sport. I was reading less but my early years at MCS was the time of *Kidnapped, Treasure Island* and Richmal Crompton's William books. These had an extra appeal as my new schoolmates now called me not Alan, my Christian name, but Wilf, Willy and Will.

We began to meet in town in the holidays. Girls were more talked about than talked to. Tex Collier may have been well ahead of most of us in this regard. Occasionally, a copy of *Heath and Efficiency* would surface. This was a magazine promoting the naturist lifestyle, though it was not the lifestyle we were interested in. *Spick* and *Span* were two magazines that boys showed around, ogling the black and white photos. Their *mise en scène* could hardly have been more banal, girls in a spray of petticoats caught in the wind or sitting demurely on a log before falling off to reveal their arousing suspenders and stocking tops. Max Harris' uncle returned from Egypt with some small photos of much more adventurous antics featuring naked men and women. In a trice, before they had been properly passed round, they were confiscated and Max was in serious trouble, as he was again soon after when he wore a sharp, tartan jacket to school and was sent home.

Our meeting places in town were one of the two Oxford music shops, Russell Acott in the High and Taphouses next to Elliston's in Magdalen Street. Both sold musical instruments on the ground floor; upstairs at Acott's and downstairs at Taphouses was the record department. In both you could ask to hear a record with a view, ahem, to buying it. The assistant would play it through to one of the glass doored booths, where we nodded our heads, tapped our toes and tried to convey the impression that we might just have recorded it ourselves. Sometimes we did buy. My first purchase was "Earth Angel" ("Will you be mine? My darling dear, love you all the time") by the Crew-Cuts, followed swiftly by "Shake Rattle and Roll" ("Well, you never do nothin' to save your doggone soul") and "Rock Around the Clock" ("Put your glad rags on and join me, hon', We'll have some fun when the clock strikes one") by Bill Haley and the Comets. It's hard to convey now the electric shock that early rock and roll music gave to the world of Mantovani's strings and Eddie Calvert's trumpet. Haley, already thirty years old, was an unlikely revolutionary with his big moon face and silly kiss curl, but his shows caused riots. In my brief newspaper career I interviewed him over tea in his dressing room on his 1964 tour. I found myself feeling sorry for him as he explained why the first house had been disappointing: his fans had to return from work before what he was sure would be a fuller second performance. After Haley came Elvis, Chuck Berry, Jerry Lee Lewis, Buddy Holly and the Everlys. We cultivated our taste listening to Alan Freed's Rock and Roll Half Hour, 9.30 Saturday evening on Radio Luxembourg: "And now, the fabulous fat man from New Orleans," and up came the jaunty "I'm walkin', Yes indeed, I'm talkin' About you and me, I'm hopin' That you'll come back to me," from Fats Domino. It was important in one's circle to be the first to hear these seminal works. I didn't always get that right, buying the bland Pat Boone's version of Little Richard's "Tutti Frutti", dried pasta rather than fresh, I think. I thought jazz might demonstrate my taste leadership. I bought 78 rpms of Johnny Dankworth and Jack Parnell on the Parlophone Super Rhythm Style series and my first LP, the *Benny Goodman Story*, after seeing the film.

The masters' common room was in a single-storey concrete building, the urinal of which compelled the teachers to gaze out through a window as they performed. Boys doffed their caps to them as they passed. There were just 24 masters for over 400 boys (today more than 120 teachers, plus twenty assistants, drama staff and technicians and nearly forty music teachers service 900 pupils in the all fee-paying school). They were an eclectic bunch. Our geography teacher was Rev "Bott" Johns, short, gruff and Welsh, who won extra respect from some of us for coaching an unbeaten first XV.

He provided a vicarious link to films, for his brother was the actor Mervyn Johns and, thus, he was uncle to the pretty, husky voiced Glynis Johns. When she appeared as Mary Tudor in *Sword and the Rose*, Tex Collier swore she wore no knickers and you could see her fanny when she danced with Richard Todd. If there had been a way of confirming this enticing news we would have found it. Bott had a temper and shouted at us. "Plug" Manwaring, an excellent chemistry teacher, had a small knobkerrie. He would patrol behind us as we sat at the laboratory benches and use it to correct one's errors by rapping out chemical compositions on the back of the head.

"Copper sulphate, Wyatt, is C (tap) u (tap) S (tap) O (tap) 4 (tap). Got it?"

"Yes Sir. Got it."

"FAG" Garside was an expert chalk thrower, when angry substituting a blackboard rubber for the chalk. He cut a dignified figure, tall with a long face, a grin never far away, and a pleasing voice that would have worked well on the radio. F.A.G. were his initials but appropriately a cigarette hung from his lower lip, a gift to the school cartoonists. Had we but known, he was a distinguished mathematician: the "Garside Theory" solving an important algorithmic problem. One summer morning the windows were open for the maths lesson in the prefabricated classroom which was his domain. While FAG was writing an equation on the blackboard, Tex Collier produced a firework and passed it to Pem, who lit it and threw it out of the window. FAG sensing a movement, turned to ask, "What was that, Pemberton?" Pem's reply "Nothing, Sir," was followed by the impressive explosion of the banger outside. The punishment FAG imposed was what one might expect from a future Mayor of Oxford. Pem had to spend an hour touring the school premises picking up litter.

I am not sure which master it was who took us on an outing to Pinewood Studios in 1955. Fun for him and fun for us, I guess. It doesn't sound like the sort of thing our form master, "Froggy" Stoneham, might have done, but I may be unfair to him. The film we saw being shot was *Man of the Moment*, a Norman Wisdom comedy. We were taken onto the studio floor and while we didn't encounter Wisdom we did meet the blonde and beautiful Belinda Lee, his co-star. I was just the right height to gaze closely at her ample bosom as she gave me her autograph. I stared unashamedly, for to my surprise the exposed upper slopes were covered in makeup. My autograph book smelled of her powder for years. If it was you, Froggy, thank you.

The idiosyncrasies of masters, the odd glimpse of bullying, the pranks and so on are just flashes of light through the vast clouds of unremembered hours and uneventful days of school. The true life of school was fixing the bike chain when it came off, packing and unpacking the satchel, the frustration of difficult homework, glee when the teacher forgot to set any, elation at completing easy questions quickly, relief at finishing the essay. It was the charge of excitement in some lessons, the dreamy boredom of others, anxiety when you just couldn't grasp something. It was answering a question in class, lifting the lever on the fountain pen causing a little gurgle as it filled with blue black, being amazed at how satisfying a geometry solution could be, testing oneself on French or Latin vocab, wondering why anyone ever spoke Greek. It was sitting at the back of the class practising and revising one's signature, selecting the England football team, memorising all 48 states of America, passing silly notes, trying to fart silently, time limping slowly through a double period on a warm afternoon. It was the hole in the stomach as you neared the team sheet on the notice board, elation at being selected, hiding disappointment when not. It was fielding practice, daft jokes in the playground, trying to impress by imitating Elvis.

History remained my favourite subject and I was fortunate to have J.S. "Sid" Millward as a teacher. It was "Sid" after a music and comedy act Sid Millward and his Nitwits. Sid was slightly pompous but a brilliant teacher. Discipline was implicit in his command of the material and the class. His lessons were impeccably organised; he pushed us to read and to think. He taught a course of American history, loved America and would show off his familiarity with its idiom by answering "Check" when an Englishman would say "Yes". To indicate when he was being ironic he would push his tongue high into his cheek in an exaggerated manner, as if demonstrating the figure of speech to the hard of hearing. His hair was a great point of speculation. It was brushed flat but a wayward strand always formed an upward curl at the rear. This we dubbed "Sidney trouble" and shouted it mockingly at any boy whose hair broke ranks in this way. We admired Sid, though like all teachers he could be mocked. Once, in the sixth form he was speculating about armies crossing the freezing Valtelline Pass between Italy and Germany during the Thirty Years War and wondered aloud how they fed themselves. "The peasants up there are so poor they could not offer more than a glass of milk in summer. What on earth would they offer in winter?" At the back Pemberton answered sotto voce and with impeccable logic, "Ice cream?" Sid left at the end of my first year in the sixth form to become a headmaster.

He talked to us about segregation in the USA and the civil rights movement which was beginning to make itself felt with bus boycotts in the South. This led him on to apartheid in South Africa. He was convinced that the country would blow up before long. The unfairness of both situations was unarguable to me. West Indian immigrants were growing in number in Britain. Television programmes told of how the new arrivals were treated. One Caribbean woman described how she could sense whites recoiling from her, how they sought to avoid touching black people. This was dreadful, I thought. One or two black bus conductresses had begun working on buses in Oxford and I resolved to do my bit to bring the races together. When I handed over my fare to one or received change I took particular care, however unnecessarily, to make sure my fingers touched her hand. They must have wondered what I was up to and talked among themselves about the strange boy with the brushing fingers. It was around then that my parents took us to have tea with "Uncle" Richard and "Auntie" Maisie. He was a college servant at Worcester College and, in spite of Dad's bricklayer scorn for "pisspot emptiers", was a friend of my parents. They lived in one of the ancient Worcester cottages that sit just below road level at the top of Walton Street. The couple had worked in the West Indies and their talk turned to how blacks were stupid and untrustworthy. You had to beware of "uppity niggers". Mixed race people, "high browns", were naturally more intelligent than full blacks but still lacking. I wouldn't listen to this quietly and began to argue. Voices were raised, a full blown row developed and we left. I didn't see them again.

The school chaplain was A.S.T. "Stan" Fisher. He was tall, lean with dark hair brushed flat across crown of his head and loped slowly about the school with his gown flowing outwards, like a large distracted wader bird. He hunched his shoulders slightly as he looked down at you through his spectacles. It was a penetrating look. He had edited a book of prayers and one of poetry and both chose and enunciated his words with care. At Christ Church, Oxford, he had been a friend of W.H. Auden who, he said, had drifted off to a grander circle after the first year. I think Stan was quite shy. By the time he led our study of *Antony and Cleopatra* in the sixth form I was aware of an inner intellectual life. In a quiet and dignified way he convinced us, almost certainly all virgins, in his analysis of the sexual passion that brought ruin and death to the Roman general and the Egyptian queen. He had us reading Joyce, Donne, Marvell, Keats and *Leaves of Grass*, Walt Whitman's free verse hymn to love, nature and the human body. Stan was eloquent on these subjects and on the creative process. He had known Michael Tippett, who told him that when he was composing he had to masturbate frequently. Well, that was one good reason, we supposed.

Before the sixth form, we considered him chiefly in the context of sex. We knew he swam at Parson's Pleasure, the male-only nude bathing place on the Cherwell. At Cowley swimming baths he wandered naked through the changing room, pulling towels away from small boys and proclaiming, "We're not shy here." Well, he wasn't. It fell to him to teach us biology in the lower fourth, the main purpose of which was to impart the facts of life while we sniggered. He was soon to publish *Happy Families – The Meaning of Sex for Young Teenagers* which he illustrated with line drawings of his children. We heard quite a bit about flowers and insects before we moved onto the main course. When we did, some dryly offered comments stirred the imagination. "During intercourse the penis is put into the vagina. It is usually moved backwards and forwards as most people find that creates a pleasant sensation." How interesting, we probably thought before returning to our sniggers. "Sir, what causes an emission of pungent gasses from the anus, Sir?" (The bum and the prick both falling into the category of the rude.) As school chaplain, Stan prepared us for confirmation. A serious one-to-one interrogation was part of this.

"Do you masturbate?"

"Um, yes, Sir."

"When you do, what do you think about or look at?"

"Pictures, Sir."

"Aah, pictures of what?"

"Um, film stars, Sir."

"Film stars?"

"Yes."

"Film stars. I see. Mmm…"

I sensed this was not the right answer for Stan. Little did I know but the previous year he had published a gay schoolboy romance under a *nom de plume*.

By my fourth year at MCS friends and I were getting above ourselves. Work deteriorated, the larking about increased. We could have floated a joint stock company in mutual admiration. In short, we were damned cocky. It came to a head when we were caught playing ball tig in the chapel and causing havoc during confirmation classes, Pem hiding in the pulpit and popping up to pull silly faces, John Martin throwing cushions at him as if Stan Fisher could not see. We learned we had been dubbed the "Collier Gang" by the staff, which was a bit hard on Terry who was not a core trouble maker. None of us liked this as I think I would have preferred it to be the Wyatt Gang, Pem the Pemberton Gang and so on.

My housemaster for Maltby, Fred Porter, head of modern languages, took action. Fred had black curly hair, a high breathy voice and the air of just having put down an avant-garde novel. To school he wore a navy beret and a long shapeless mac, on his jacket a Campaign for Nuclear Disarmament badge and he let it be known he was a member of the Communist Party. He tackled us outside the chapel door, giving us a dressing down, then summoned us to see him one by one. His tone with me indicated that he was irritated by all this and yet was confiding.

"The Collier Gang is becoming a pain in the school. Did you know that, laddie?"

"No, Sir."

"Well, it is I can assure you. You are not stupid, Wyatt. You could do well."

"I'm sorry, Sir."

Then the blow to the solar plexus. "If you go on like this, laddie, you'll end up selling matches on a street corner. Do you know that?"

"No, Sir."

"Think about it."

It sounds rather mild now. No shouting, no histrionics and no other threats but it worked for me. I was shaken and felt guilty. My parents had left school at fourteen, my father was working tiringly hard, my mother had thrown herself into supporting her sons. All this was getting back to them. I was ashamed.

I was forever grateful to Fred for the way he handled me. He was an archetypal North Oxford intellectual, utterly different from my background, but I respected him. He had been a friend of Kingsley Amis and told me how once Amis had rung him to say that he couldn't get back to Swansea and could he stay the night with Fred and his wife? He slept in the spare room and said his goodbyes the following morning. Next to his bed was a ceramic bedside light and when Mrs Porter went to change the sheets, the bed nudged the side table very slightly and the lamp fell in pieces. Examining it, she could see that Amis must have smashed the lamp and, in an act worthy of the burnt sheets scene in *Lucky Jim*, had reassembled it with immense care so that it just balanced until he disappeared from the house, knowing discovery would be inevitable.

Fred sensed his A level French pupils had much to learn about life as they studied Corneille: "This is real sexual passion, laddie, not just a Tudor constitutional document." He liked to shock us rather straight-laced teenagers.

"Do you know what I saw last night? I was driving down Broad Street, and there, at the corner of Turl Street, I saw one of my Maltby mums, necking - or do you laddies say snogging?" He paused and looked round the classroom. "And not with anyone I recognised."

When I left school, dear Fred took a few of us out for a beer and dispensed advice, "Lots of girls around, you know. Have plenty of sex."

After Fred's boot to my backside, a power surge propelled my work and ambitions in the O Level year. Mum had awarded these public examinations "golden ball" status, a chance not to be dropped. To that end she confiscated my records so I wouldn't waste time listening to them rather than working. I hid a few treasured ones between some books but when I went to retrieve them to listen to when she was out I was caste down to find them broken by the pressure. Magdalen itself was pressing me forwards. The teachers, the destinations of senior boys, the academic work comprised an on-stage chorus beckoning me towards the world of the university. And a new master arrived to add to add to the general liveliness of the place.

Chris Bishop was the school's first full-time music teacher. I was not a musician but his influence spread widely. He was young and energetic with a dimpled chin and rosebud mouth leading via a long straight nose to a domed forehead.

Slightly fey in manner and wry in expression, he might just have stepped off the stage. He took us for English O Level and liked to end the lesson with two or three chords on the piano, as if concluding a Handel recitative. *Macbeth* was on the syllabus and Bishop brought a reel to reel tape recorder into the class and had us record and play back speeches from the plays. Cutting edge stuff, we thought. I recorded "Is this a dagger that I see before me, the handle toward my hand?" with a liberal sprinkling of gasps, sighs and other audible punctuation. He set us homework to produce articles as if from a current newspaper or magazine. I wrote a spoof fashion page from *Vogue* complete with illustrations, along with a pretentious recipe column and a supposed satirical political report. He loved this sort of stuff and forecast I would become a humorous columnist, people asking, "Have you read Willy this week?" I lapped this up as I was beginning to read the Peter Simple column (the Wyatts had promoted themselves from the *Express* to the *Telegraph*) peopled by J. Bonington Jagworth, of the Motorists' Liberation Front, Mrs Dutt-Pauker, the Hampstead thinker, grandmother of Bert Brecht Mao Che Oginga Odinga Dutt-Pauker, and Dr Spacely-Trellis, "the go-ahead Bishop of Bevingdon". Alas, Chris Bishop's encouraging prophecy did not come to pass.

Under Bishop, the school's music grew in ambition as he established a second orchestra, staged performances of a Purcell opera and *The Pirates of Penzance* as well as *Messiah* and *St. John Passion*, the latter recorded and a vinyl long player sold in the school. He started a band for the Combined Cadet Force. When the BBC televised a live studio production of Verdi's *Otello*, Bishop was in the chorus and we spotted him whirling in the cheering crowd. He went on to make things happen in the music business as he had at MCS, producing great recordings with Barbirolli, Previn, Giulini and others before managing the Philharmonia Orchestra.

When the O Level golden balls fell, there was no Mr Gray around to assist. By then I am confident I would have taken a different stance. I never cheated in an exam again, if you don't count one or two history dates written on my wrist for Tripos papers. As it was, I dropped only one of the nine I took. If you were in the top set for maths you also had to sit the additional maths paper and during the year I realised I had walked into a wall. The moment arrived when we were being taught differential calculus and the master said, "We'll make x (or was it y?) a very small number tending to zero, so let's say that x is zero." This was too much for my pedestrian brain. It was either zero or it was not. Thereafter, I was among the walking wounded. Not long ago, I recited this failure to a professor of mathematics, who replied, "A lot of people have trouble with that," not quite adding, "but quickly get over it."

I was heading for what was then not called "uni". No one ever asked me what my "passion" was. There was no talk of "following your dream". I wasn't expected to map out my "goals". Life proceeded in an orderly fashion. I had always enjoyed history, was good at it and, thus, it would be my chief A Level. I chose English Literature as my second subject and had no say in the third. In those days, a history candidate for both Oxford and Cambridge had to sit a Latin translation paper. The school deemed that I was such a candidate but that my Latin was too poor to retain the necessary standard in two years' time so told me that I should take Latin A Level; that way at least I might maintain a reasonable level. I was not keen to continue with Latin but I was led to a trough and instructed to drink.

David happily had now come to join me at Magdalen on a paid place. He took the eleven plus at MCS but was badly ill with jaundice and tonsillitis on the day. Mum summoned the doctor who said he should get up to take the exam and then go straight back to bed, not the best of circumstances. There was no Mr Gray to haul him over the wall. David passed well enough and was offered a place at City of Oxford High School but wanted to remain at MCS with me. Dad rang Bob Stanier, a place came vacant and David was in and soon making his mark.

Played thirteen, won thirteen. Centre row from left: Richard Warnock, WW, Alan Pemberton, Robert "Sherb" Herbertson, Terry "Tex" Collier.

12

"LOUISE HAD THE RIGHT IDEA"

was in the exciting turbulence of teenage years, a time of new enthusiasms, false starts, reverses and small triumphs. I was lucky enough - it hadn't been only luck - to be at a school which offered the sensation of living several concurrent lives, lives which interwove and at times compensated for each other. A win on the rugby field followed by another Saturday evening at home; discovering of a new poet after a dispiriting essay mark; a part in the play but love not just unrequited, unnoticed. I had been a slow developer, my voice didn't break till I was fifteen, and now I was growing bigger and stronger to the benefit of my sporting ability. I was finding new interests and adding new friends. I enjoyed the academic work in English and history. My feathers were being preened and I knew the destination of my flight.

The history teacher who did so much to put an edge on me and many others was Peter Arnold-Craft. He had served as a flight lieutenant in the RAF, then taken a first in history and won a tennis blue at Oxford. He was red haired, slight and whippety of build, straight-backed in posture and fastidious in manner. "Craft" was a tough disciplinarian who could be cruel to slower or lazier boys, but his ruddy face often twinkled and a trace of Yorkshire coloured his voice, which teased as well as scolded. In the lower fourth he described his anguish at being blooded by the hunt as a boy in North Yorkshire. This led into him making us argue the case for hunting as he attacked it. Next lesson, we had to put the case against while he shot holes in our arguments.

The A Level syllabus was the Tudors and Stuarts for English History, with hallowed texts *England Under the Tudors* by G.R. Elton, *The King's Peace* and *The King's War* by C.V. Wedgwood; for European History, we studied the comparable period with *Renaissance and Reformation* by V.H.H. Green our bible. For each subject I had two brown cardboard folders, the loose leaves threaded with laces, one for notes, the second for collected essays. I wrote my essays on a small repro davenport in my bedroom. I worked hard. Arnold-Craft was a teacher you desperately wanted to please: he pushed, cajoled and inspired. I was apprehensive when he handed back an essay. In red biro he added comments, corrections and notes throughout with a summing up and overall mark at the end. A beta double plus was a high mark; a touch of alpha and the spirit soared; too often there were plain betas, even beta minus or, disaster, beta/gamma. The overall appraisals prodded sharply: "good if garbled work"; "I am thoroughly tired of this slapdash style of yours and you are a clod for doing so little about it"; "Keep trying to avoid the pedestrian expressions you so love"; "Style: until you improve this you cannot rise above average"; "Only glimpses of your ability shown"; "Very competent but more precision and bite..."; "Quite impressive but..."; "Well argued but..." One shocker for me was when his young disabled daughter, Louise, scribbled in red biro all over the first page of one of my essays. "Sorry about this, Louise got at it I'm afraid," he wrote at the top. On the final page, after a blizzard of critical comments, Arnold-Craft concluded, "I think Louise had the right idea about this piece of work." Ouch!

He was later headmaster of Gravesend Grammar School, where he once offered me a job. He moved to be head of the Liverpool Bluecoat School for twenty-one years, saving the school from the wrecking plans of the militant Labour council and transforming the academic performance of its boys. He was co-editor with J.S. Millward of books of sixteenth-, seventeenth- and eighteenth-century portraiture and documents. No two of his pupils ever meet without his name arising.

He and Millward were the officers in charge of the RAF section of the Combined Cadet Force. From our fourth year in the school Thursday afternoons were turned over to this military training, for which we wore uniform. All were in the army section for the first year or two, then some could opt for the RAF section. Mum washed my CCF shirt but I would spend much of a Wednesday evening ironing the shirt, separate collar and tie, pressing the blouson and trousers to accentuate the creases, blancoing the gaiters and polishing boots. I enjoyed the marching: when the platoon found a crisp, synchronous rhythm it was as if we were taken over by an external force. Better still was learning to fire a 303 Lee Enfield rifle at the firing range, painful though the first recoils were. It was the standard issue rifle in both world wars of the British Army, whose heroic deeds I had read so much about.

Twice a year we would have field day. The army section was dropped in the countryside to trail around muddy fields and woods as part of an assault plan, firing blanks and shouting. We trudged back to the waiting coaches with little idea as to whether we were victors or the defeated. The first time I spent a night away from my parents was at the CCF summer camp at Windmill Hill, Wiltshire, in July 1957. I remember it being hot, the marches long and a blistered itchy rash on my arm. My cards home tell what was on my mind, "...the food is still pretty good and I am not hungry at the moment. We have to do our kit before 8.30, then we go out training until about 4 with a break for lunch. After tea at 4.30 or 5 (a hot meal) we are free. I usually go to the cinema which is free and shows only army films, to the NAAFI or I read." It doesn't sound too testing. Some boys had opted for a Naval Air base where one awoke at night to find a resident sailor with his arm under the blanket fondling his genitals. The sailor reassured him, "It's all right. I'm the Leading Hand."

I chose to move into the RAF section. It felt chicer, the blue uniform looked stylish and the masters in charge were the younger, smarter ones I related to. Sid and Craft were joined here by a new master Dave Curtis, a big, pugnacious looking geography teacher with a slightly adenoidal voice. The three of them were chums. Curtis made quite an impact on the school. He was a keen sportsman, cheerful with a matey, disarming laugh but easily slighted. He was sensitive about his apparently clumsy demeanour and flew into a temper if he thought he was being mocked in any way, notably when after a trip to Germany he thought a boy referred to him as "dummkopf". Hence, we were a touch wary although we liked him as a great supporter of us sporty boys.

When the Corps band was introduced I thought I would try to join. I played no instrument as my half-hearted desire to become a second Benny Goodman had fizzled out on the lower slopes of learning the recorder, so I auditioned as a drummer. If not Benny, I thought, then perhaps Gene Krupa, another member of Goodman's wonderful quartet. Millward and Arnold-Craft intervened, implying that the band was a louche option and they had other plans for me.

One of the attractions of the RAF section had been flying. I should have known better. I had been queasy on the holiday flight to Dinan from Bournemouth, a temporary aberration I must have thought after all those books about RAF heroes. Not so. On field days and camps at RAF stations I only need sniff the rubbery smell of a military plane interior to feel nauseous and fifteen minutes in the air would cause me to throw up. I filled the thick brown paper bags in a de Havilland Chipmunk, an Avro Anson, a Vickers Valetta, a Blackburn Beverley transport plane, a Gloster Meteor T7 fighter and, most impressively of all, a Gloster NF-11 night fighter. In the Chipmunk the pilot asked, "Have you tried a stall turn before?" The only truthful answer was "No", and before I could add any caveat we were lurching up and then swooping down. On each flight I hoped that my air legs would grow steady but it was not to be. I think I avoided a flight when we spent time at RAF Scampton, former home of the Dam Busters, then base for Avro Vulcan V bombers. The highlight here was seeing a shiny atom bomb wheeled out on a trailer to be loaded in a Vulcan's bomb bay. I was not yet in my CND phase so while I wondered at how much destruction this modestly sized weapon held, I was reassured that we really did have them.

Later in that summer of 1958 a small miracle occurred when a group of us flew to Germany for a stay at RAF Laarbruch: thanks to some travel pills I survived two and a quarter hours in a Vickers Varsity without being sick. We had a great time on the station's shooting range firing not just Bren guns but pistols and the new Sterling submachine gun, capable of 600 rounds per minute. We were put up in the officers' mess, the etiquette of which was sternly impressed on us before we left. It was all to my taste as a letter home testifies: "We had a meal when we arrived then the Orderly Officer virtually forced us into the bar to say hello to the Group Captain. He is a big chap with a red face, nothing like the bloke at Scampton. This morning I was woken up with a cup of tea by a German batwoman… This afternoon a Canberra made a crash landing but no-one was injured. Tomorrow I shall probably be going up in a Canberra…" I don't think I did.

We saw a little of Germany, glad that our bombers had missed the towers of Cologne cathedral and surprised at the amount of smart new building as we drove through Düsseldorf. We won the war, didn't we? We made a trip into the Netherlands to pay homage to the bridge at Arnhem, the bold typeface of our understanding on the "heroic" rather than "failure" aspect of the story. At the base,

I developed a teenage boy's taste for lager and lime and on return talked knowingly about the Liebfraumilch we were offered in the mess. We wore a suit for dinner each evening and I had with me a black clip on bow tie for the promised formal dinner. Dave Curtis got into quite a tizz when he inspected us before this do. Horror of horrors, some of us had only grey not black socks to wear; did we not know that black was the form for such occasions? Insecurity was on display here. Surely the mess would not have bothered about us boys, but perhaps Dave was worrying lest the Group Captain thought he was the oik who knew no better?

A second kind of corps camp, "arduous training", was introduced in the Easter holiday by another new master, Bob Holmes, who was MCS' first Physical Education teacher. In came proper PE for all forms, mats, vaults, ropes, fencing and circuit training for rugby. He was an enthusiast and a thoroughly good thing. But we took to him only slowly, partly because he tried to be too matey - he called Richard Warnock "Dickie", a familiar never applied hitherto - and partly out of snobbery. In a common room of masters from Oxford and Cambridge universities, he had studied at Loughborough College and had an easily imitable northern accent. Bob Holmes, quite dapper with a little moustache, won us round with his eagerness and optimism.

I enjoyed the corps. I liked the drill. I enjoyed the flight simulators in which I could fly and land a bomber without the penalty of leaving the ground. My dislike of the actual purpose of the RAF, the flying, did not hold me back and I floated up the ranks to become under officer and head of the corps. Wearing the red sash of command, I took the parade each week shouting orders and swaggering about, confessing to my diary that I "enjoyed strutting with my cane". What is more, my exalted rank allowed me to dispense with boots and gaiters and wear ordinary black shoes with my uniform. In retrospect, I'm not sure how valuable the CCF was. The discipline might have been useful when National Service loomed until the late fifties, but my vintage missed it by a couple of years. At least one prominent academic parent took Stanier aside to tell him it was "an organised waste of time" and by the time my brother's turn came he was able to opt out.

Back at the real work of school, the A Level English syllabus included Milton's masque, *Comus*, *Antony and Cleopatra* and a second Shakespeare, *Coriolanus*, for which our clever and imaginative guide was Robert Avery. He had been a boy at the school and now returned as a master. Though still in his early twenties, he was bald and slightly stooped and with our recent study of *Volpone* in mind, we identified him in his black gown, physically at least, as a character from that play, Signor Voltore, Mr Vulture. Somebody said of his pale looks, "Mr Avery of the ivory ovary". He was far from vulture-like in other ways, serious and inspiring in his teaching, already cast as something of an eccentric with a vintage Rolls Royce and a passion for steam railways. He was an enthusiastic cricketer, a left arm spin bowler, the only person I knew who bowled as slowly and with as high a trajectory as Bob Stanier.

Avery was a man of the theatre and transmitted his own excitement to his pupils. Television provided me with a supply of great plays, Ibsen, Sherriff, Anouilh, Shaw, Dodie Smith and even N.F. Simpson. It was a time when British theatre was afire with new voices, new ideas and new language. I had persuaded my parents to take us to see the Ilfracombe summer repertory theatre perform *Look Back in Anger*, a notorious play, the newspapers said. I loved the vituperative outpourings of Jimmy Porter which chimed with my developing view of the world. I saw the film of this, and two other movies in the same appealing key, adaptations not of plays but novels, *Room at the Top* and *Saturday Night and Sunday Morning*. At the Oxford Playhouse I saw and was excited by Joan Littlewood's production of *Macbeth* set in a dictatorship in the era of the First World War. Even more thrilling in a quite different genre was the London stage production of *West Side Story* that a friend and I made a special trip to see. Avery prompted one or two of us to go to another Playhouse production, *The Bacchae*, starring Yvonne Mitchell and a Scottish actor we knew from television and films, Sean Connery, still three years away from becoming James Bond. Avery was an enthusiastic admirer of Samuel Beckett, whom he had met, and read *Waiting for Godot* with us. The play's opaqueness was no bother; this was like nothing else, a prank, a whimsical joke we didn't quite get but were flattered to be party to. A year or so later Robert Avery asked Alan Pemberton and me to play Estragon and Vladimir in what was to be the first amateur production of the play but we had plans to leave a term early and others had this honour.

My third subject was Latin, as already explained. Tam Swann was our teacher, a thoroughly decent man who deserved better than me and one or two of my classmates. He was tall and well-built, though with hunched shoulders around which a long woollen scarf was wound for most of the year. I wince remembering how as senior boys we behaved in his class: "Who's that funny old man talking to himself?", one would ask loud enough for him to hear as he explained a subtlety of Virgil's verse in his low voice. "You bloody boy!" he would shout in one of his occasional outbursts, often accompanying it with a cuff round a head with his open hand. We felt bad about exasperating him as we liked him, but not bad enough to cease amusing each other at his expense. I now resent the time spent on Latin O and A Levels. The syllabus was entirely concerned with the language, of which I retain next to nothing. I was not the dimmest and would have relished learning about classical civilisation or Roman history but they were ignored. Whenever I have complained about this, the answer has usually been that Latin was so important for what it contributed to the English language. In which case, a fortnightly lesson in prefixes, suffixes and roots would have served and time released to study the other important legacies of Rome.

Robert Avery was co-director of the annual Shakespeare production. I see now how he made this a lesson in casting to type. In 1958, for *Coriolanus*, he turned the behaviour of the so-called Collier Gang to good use and cast us as the unruly citizens of Rome. Proud Coriolanus himself was the tight-lipped head of the boarding house, A.J. Cole, and the elder Pye, Graham, with aristocratic drawl and a haughty air was cast as his nemesis Tullus Aufidius. Volumnia, Coriolanus' mother, was the fresh faced Tim Hunt, somewhat tall for the role but he spoke the verse with perfect diction in his soft, velvety voice. I had a line or two as a citizen and was grateful for being hauled into such an enjoyable enterprise. The tiny stage of Big School allowed for nothing as spectacular as the conclusion of the performance we saw on a first visit to Stratford the following year. Laurence Olivier as Coriolanus was stabbed to death on a high platform falling backwards to hang suspended upside down.

Next year Avery had to find an Antony and a Cleopatra. The latter was a junior boy I didn't know; Antony had to be the school's best actor, John "Tich" Davies. He had a big, round expressive face, a slight Welsh accent and loved an argument at which he was both passionate and eloquent. His father was the several times unsuccessful Liberal candidate for the Oxford parliamentary seat.

Tich won the annual recitation competition more than once, memorably with "Naming of Parts" by Henry Reed. The poem alternates a military lecture on using a rifle with dreamy thoughts of nature, and Tich found both the humour and the poignancy, shifting the direction of his stance as he moved between the two voices. He had to be Antony but there was a problem: Antony is a mighty general, a military hero, and Tich a spindly non-sporty boy. He began coming to school with large bags of nuts which he ate by the handful. He had, he told us, signed up for a Charles Atlas body building course. Advertisements for this were everywhere in the newspapers, magazines and comics. They showed the immense shiny torso of Charles Atlas gleaming with strength and wellbeing. Alongside was a drawing of a fearful-looking skinny youth and the exhortation, "Don't be a seven-stone weakling, don't let them kick sand in your face." The answer was the secret of "Dynamic Tension" and, evidently, a nut filled diet. After several weeks of this regime the dress rehearsal arrived. Alas, when Tich slipped on his cardboard armour to play Antony, "triple pillar of the world", his arm stuck out as a broom handle through a port hole. It didn't matter; few boys would have spoken the verse better. I had some lines as Agrippa. Tim Hunt had the great "Age shall not wither her..." speech as Enobarbus. Tich went on to star in Oxford Union debates and in 1987 stood for Labour against Mrs Thatcher in her Finchley constituency, making a small dent in her majority.

The school was now part of me. I was aware that the world was opening up in an exciting way and was a conventional soul, loyal to the institution that was enabling this. When the government proposed a new inner relief road for the city to run through the boarding house across our playing field and Christ Church Meadow, I shared the outrage of Bob Stanier and the teaching staff. It was an assault on my world. Good sense prevailed and the route was first changed and eventually abandoned. My devotion to the school was nowhere more manifest than on the playing fields, though not at every sport. For a long while I couldn't become enthusiastic about hockey and considered the Hilary term a time to have Wednesday and Saturday afternoons for myself. The school was strong at the game and my friends Richard Warnock and John Martin outstanding players, Richard captaining England schoolboys, both winning Oxford blues. Eventually, I applied myself and got into the second XI though the sport never ran in my blood.

I was never an athlete and dreaded the annual cross country run in which all had to take part. The term "cross country" was hardly appropriate. Junior, intermediate and senior courses all finished in Christ Church Meadow, the first two after a run along the Thames. The senior course would today land the organisers in court for child abuse. It began off the Botley Road and ran up and along Harcourt Hill before descending to Hinksey, a route that had us crossing traffic on the A34 Oxford Southern bypass not once but twice. We continued over Hinksey lake via the long pedestrian bridge to Abingdon Road, turning north before crossing this busy road to finish up the Broad Walk of the Meadow. If there were casualties, they were hushed up. If I couldn't run, I could swim and when inter-house swimming sports were introduced at Temple Cowley pool, I won the backstroke. The swimming competition provided a stage for Terry "Tex" Collier to strut his stuff. He had been a club swimmer for years and won several events, pulling off a true Tex stunt in the concluding staff versus school relay. By the time he was cued to swim the final leg, the school was well in the lead but he stood sweeping back his hair on the edge of the pool until the masters caught up and he could race Dave Curtis one to one, humiliating him by the ease of his victory.

Collier was wicket keeper for the first cricket XI and I had reinvented myself as an off-spin bowler. I could turn the ball, though was prone to dropping it short. After a season in the seconds I was promoted to the firsts and just about held my own. Whether or not you take the view that cricket is a team game played by individuals or an individual's game played by teams, you are exposed at important moments: when the ball is in the air and you are under it, when you breathe deeply to calm yourself as you walk out to bat. I was a nervous batsman and scored few runs. I loved fielding, usually in the covers or at short leg. I took a lot of catches in the latter position but I can only remember a chance I dropped. Most of our fixtures were afternoon games but we played one or two all-day matches, among them King's School, Worcester. On arrival, we bragged shamelessly about how we had not been beaten by a school for two years and so on. They batted first and I put down a sharp chance from one of their openers when he was in single figures. He went on to make a century, and the team a big score. We just hung on to scrape a draw. I did manage to catch a humdinger just off the ground at square leg against the old boys, particularly gratifying as that was the biggest crowd of the year, parents, siblings and even some girls. I managed to take ten wickets in my first season, enough to have my average included in the school's 1959 Wisden entry. It stood alongside far better players, notably John Martin our fast bowler who captained Oxford University. Our efforts were recorded with exemplary neatness and interrogated to provide detailed averages and analyses by our scorer, Tim Hunt. He was important enough to the side to be included in the team photos.

Happy afternoons were lost in in the rhythms and rituals of cricket on our lovely playing field: fielding practice in a wide arc as Tam Swann hit us ground shots and high catches, fierce competitive sessions on the slip cradle, experimenting with fast bowling or leg spinners in the nets, changing into jock strap and whites in a dressing room that reeked of past teams whose photos lined the pavilion walls, studs catching the pitted wooden floor, gathering to sing our team song before trooping onto the field, "Oo ee oo ah ah, ting tang walla walla bing bang; oo ee oo ah ah ting tang walla walla bing bang." Often we swam in the Cherwell afterwards, Tex and I once swimming right round the island that was the playing field.

There was no coaching as such, just general guidance and exhortation from Tam Swann, the cricket master. At the end of the summer term he and his wife Nancy gave a party for the team at their house on Woodstock Road. We played boisterous games and ate from a generous buffet. The kindly Nancy provided a home for boys and masters who fell ill and needed some care in their recovery. Tam died a few years later, enough years I hope that our dreadful behaviour in sixth form Latin had not hastened his end. Nancy was to be 39 years a widow.

Eric "Smokey" Summers, biology master, was in charge of the first rugby XV but by far the greatest influence on the team and its success was our hooker and "Captain of Rugger" for two years, an unusual honour in itself, Alan Pemberton. He did not just inspire our spirit and resolve, but berated failings, commanded moves and shaped our tactics. Short, strong and ferocious in combat, Pem was a skilful ball player. His one weakness was being short-sighted. This mattered little on the pitch but tripped him up elsewhere. As captain Pem was first one off the coach when we arrived at an away fixture and at Worcester he greeted a waiting figure, shook his hand and exclaimed,

"Congratulations, skipper this year I see."

The reply was, "No, no, I'm the coach driver who's just driven you here."

I was Hon. Sec. for the second year, confirming the fixtures, ensuring oranges were provided at half time and organising Crappers Coaches. The great game when travelling to and from an away match was to kneel on the back seat looking out at cars behind. One of us would pretend to spot something wrong with the following vehicle and begin an elaborate charade of nudging a colleague to draw his attention to this, beginning a chain reaction of concerned faces, nodding heads and pointing fingers. When the following driver's attention was captured we would furrow brows and make increasingly anxious wobbly wheel gestures. The object, and successes were not that rare, was to get the driver behind to stop and examine his car, only to discover nothing was wrong.

Our rugby fixture list included local rivals, Southfield, Abingdon and City of Oxford High School. I wonder if their team ever included a boy who had very nearly passed the eleven plus well enough to get into Magdalen? In 1960 we beat everyone including Bradford Grammar School (13-0), who were on tour, and in the final match, three days before Christmas, Ampleforth College (6-5, two tries to a converted try), who were unbeaten in the north of England and came down to play us. In those days, *The Daily Telegraph* carried school rugby results which we scoured throughout the term to see who was doing well. Both it and *The Times* had a schools' rugby correspondent. The latter carried a full report of the Ampleforth match, sealing, as we saw it, our status as champs: played thirteen, won thirteen. The most memorable score was against a very strong old boys' side when "Tex", a dashing centre, was flip tackled, completed a somersault only to regain his feet and coolly drop a goal to win the match. We did have several top players: Nigel Starmer-Smith won an Oxford blue and played for England; Mick Simmie also a blue and a trial for Scotland; Robert Herbertson won an England trial.

We were full of ourselves and a touch pompous, suffering the conceit that the rest of the school should come to watch, to cheer, to admire. Some did. The triumphant season left me with a feeling of pride and a cauliflower ear, swollen and sore from scrummaging. I went to Dr Stewart, a big jolly man who had, I think, been a player himself. Looking at it, he said, "Yes. What happens is that with all the rubbing against the opposing prop it blows up and fills with blood. We have to try to get rid of that." He made a painful incision in the swelling with what looked like a Stanley knife and instructed me to squeeze the blood out though it twice a day. This should limit the disfigurement, he said. "When you are a rich businessman, you can pay for cosmetic surgery to put it right." Squeeze I did for a fortnight, screwing up my face at the pain. The ear still looks a little odd but I came to consider it a war wound.

After the penultimate game of the season against the old boys, in true rugby fashion the men took the boys to the Eastgate pub in the High to drink beer. Cheeks reddened, eyes brightened and rude songs were sung. The previous year's gathering was when I was first drunk. After an intake of no more than two or three pints, I had set off to cycle home with Sherb, neither of us with front lights. The little black battery lamps that fitted onto a bracket below the handle bars were always disappearing. We were steady enough, I thought, and there were few cars about on a cold evening. As we approached Summertown a policeman stepped off the pavement to intercept us. Befuddled, I pulled hard at both front and rear brakes and found myself staring up at the policeman having fallen off at his feet. He didn't laugh, at least not to my face.

"Where is your front light?"

I told the truth, "Um, stolen I think."

"Then you should not be riding on the road in this way. How far do you have to go?"

"Just past the roundabout. Sunderland Avenue".

With a gesture of his head he indicated we could go on, "You'd better walk the rest of the way."

Sherb and I walked past the parade of shops, up the slight rise where the large Masonic Lodge sat back behind trees, to where he turned off. Sherb lived in Southdale Road on the middle-class side of the Cutteslowe Walls, several streets of modest semi-detached houses built privately in the early thirties. The developer had constructed eight-foot-high walls with spikes on top to block movement between his private estate and the council estate next door. As we made our uncertain way home in December 1959, it was only months since the walls had been finally demolished. I continued walking to the roundabout, turned left into Sunderland Avenue, then along the service road past Uncle Walter and Mrs H's jumbo-sized house ("It's rated a mansion by the electricity board," she told us) and finally home. As I pushed open the side gate I was feeling pretty nauseous. I knew what the trouble was and resolved that very moment that I would never drink beer again.

WW as Thomas Horner
about to fight the apprentice.

13
IN MY HEAD AND IN MY UNDERSTANDING

Out of school I was not overburdened with chores. The first time I made my own bed was when I went to CCF camp, otherwise it was my mother who sorted the sheets, blankets and eiderdown that comprised bedding in those days. In the holidays it was my job always to hoover the stairs. I did some washing up, digging in the garden, helped clean the car and in the holidays some regular office work for Dad. Pretty cushy really. I never had a paper round of my own but for several years I stood in for friends who did when they were ill or away. The paper shop was in Summertown owned and run by Mr Bird, who shouted and charged about every morning as if he was responsible for launching D-Day but had mislaid the maps. His face would redden amidst the piles of marked up papers and we feared for his health, a heart attack but one absent delivery boy away. Once I'd got the hang of balancing the heavy bag of papers on my handlebars, I enjoyed the round. It was surprisingly easy to get up at 6, it was exhilarating to be out and about early both in the winter dark, which made one feel a bit of a hero, and on the bright summer mornings. Mind you, I only did this now and then. Best of all was the smell of the accumulated newsprint first thing. I still love the smell of a newspaper. Like the warm, biscuit scent of a library, it is a smell of promised pleasure.

I was becoming good friends with two boys from the non-sporty, artistic wing of my cohort and casting off into the waters of a different social world. Non-sporty is a bit hard on Tim Hunt as he was an enthusiastic scorer for the first cricket XI and in this role travelled with the team but he didn't play. He, too, was in the RAF section and in my houseroom. Tim, whose first school had been the mixed tiddlers' section of the Girls High School and then the Dragon, was tall but very boyish in looks and manner and played the French horn in the school orchestra. We didn't study together as he was a scientist, primarily a biologist (he had dissected his brother's pet rabbit when it died) but he liked paintings and was a keen photographer. We both liked modern architecture, the excitement of the new, and were more impressed than it deserved by Oxford's first modernist construction, the Hume-Rothery Building in Parks Road. Tim's father Richard was a mediaevalist and Keeper of Western Manuscripts at the Bodleian Library, tall, thoughtful and gently spoken. Kit, his mother, was short, stocky and energetic. She cooked Tim Christmas pudding for his birthday in February because it was his favourite pudding. Kit referred to me as "Tim's Teddy Boy friend". I was never close to being a "Ted", who were by then passé, but as my mother's son I was a relatively snappy dresser, whereas the Hunts were an academic old tweed jacket and woolly jumper family. Also, I was from a town family and if not from the wrong side of the tracks, then at least from outside the college gates.

This friendship was a first-hand introduction to the customs of a household similar to that of my mother's employers, Dr and Mrs Heaton, customs I would seek to emulate. In 1960 the Hunts invited me for Boxing Day supper to their terraced house in Walton Street. This was unusual. My other friends and I didn't spend much time in each other's houses, calling in just to join up for an outing; meals were rare to non-existent. I had tea at Pem's once and I recall lunch at the Presbyterian Herbertson table where his father said grace. That was about it. So supper, and on a feast day, was a first. We had spent that Christmas in Newbury with Phyl and Ron and to leave the family gathering was seen as quite a statement, a stride into a different milieu. I caught a bus back to Oxford to reach the Hunts for 7.30. Tim's two brothers were there and it was a happy gathering. The meal is where my lower middle-class manners blundered into the rituals of the academic middle classes. After a helping of cold turkey and other Boxing Day treats, the large serving plate was passed towards me and Mrs Hunt asked," Would you like some more?" Now in our house you had a damn great plateful of grub and that was that. So I said, "No thank you. That was delicious" or some such. All the Hunts proceeded to have a second helping. By now I had twigged this was the done thing but pride wouldn't allow me to ask for a second helping, thereby revealing I had got it all wrong when trying to be on my best behaviour. I have rarely refused a second helping since.

A second newer friendship was with another ex-Dragon boy, John Cooke, a fellow historian. "Cookie" had an intimate conversational manner, a professorial air and was a fount of knowledge on Germany, architecture and much else. He was full of good humour and liked making complicated jokes at which he was not ashamed to laugh himself. His father whom he referred to as "A.H." was A.H. Cooke, physicist and later Warden of New College. John's mother, a German Jewish refugee, whose English was still coloured by her native tongue, was warmly welcoming to me. The family lived in a large detached house in Savile Road, a cul de sac in the middle of the city. It pleased John to know that the house lay just within the civil war defences of Oxford. His maternal grandmother lived with them. Granny Sachs, a tiny, very feminine woman with a strong German accent, had been brought up in a well-to-do Berlin household in the last years of the nineteenth century and had her way of doing things. Her room was just to the left inside the front door of the house. When she spotted me - and no doubt others - coming up the path from the gate she stationed herself just inside the front door, enabling her to intercept and usher me into her room for a glass of Cinzano, a favourite of hers that soon became a favourite with me. "Now, Vill, come this way. Tell me vot you have been doing." It wasn't quite a salon but she liked to keep up with the young and was enormous fun.

I was beginning to take myself seriously, not least concerning "cinema" as I began to call it. I was stirred by Hollywood morality tales - *Twelve Angry Men* and *The Defiant Ones*, and British social comment - *Room at the Top*, *I'm Alright Jack* and *Saturday Night and Sunday Morning*. I began reviewing films in a notebook and raised my sights from *Picturegoer* and *Film Review* to a subscription to *Sight and Sound*. I began to understand how the best directors stamped their films with a recognisable artistic signature: John Ford - *The Searchers*, *Stagecoach*, *The Horse Soldiers*; Alfred Hitchcock - *North by Northwest*, *Vertigo*, *Psycho*; Billy Wilder - *Some Like It Hot*, *The Apartment*. I absorbed lines that stay forever: "That'll be the day"; "That's the way it crumbles, cookie wise"; "That's funny, that plane's dustin' crops where there ain't no crops."

Then came subtitles, very important in that one was often put off a British or American film by clunky dialogue whereas French or Italian dialogue, especially when not understood, was full of significance and romance. François Truffaut's *Les Quatre Cent Coups* touched my heart with its story and excited me with its freewheeling style. *Hiroshima Mon Amour* may have nudged me towards CND. I watched *L'Avventura* reverently, clearly a masterpiece because all the right people said so, but it was hard to be unaware that not much happened. More, however, than in Peter Brook's *Moderato Cantabile*. I even admitted to myself that I found it a bore. Jean-Luc Godard was more like it, *À Bout de Souffle* flew off the screen with energy, humour and Jean Seberg and Visconti hit me in the solar plexus with *Rocco and His Brothers*. Buñuel touched me elsewhere with his steamy

The Young One and *Viridiana*, foot fetish, crown of thorns, the last supper and all. The notebook began to fill and I hadn't yet discovered Ingmar Bergmann.

On television, the Wyatts were still marooned on BBC island with our single channel set. Thus, I was unable to join school talk about *Dragnet*, *Take Your Pick* or *Sunday Night at the Palladium* but I couldn't get enough of the smart American comedies shown on the BBC, *Jack Benny*, *Burns and Allen*, *The Dick van Dyke Show* and *Sergeant Bilko*. America was the promised land, cars the size of a back garden and skyscrapers. To watch the comedies was more than just enjoyment; it proposed me for the ranks of those who might one day go there.

The BBC also provided my evening classes. On Monday nights, the mighty talents of Robin Day, John Morgan and Robert Kee reported in *Panorama*. I was hypnotised and also getting above myself. Dad would drop off alongside me as he watched with a bottle of beer by his side. I fumed within at his negligence. How could he sleep through this improving stuff? What sort of a man could ignore this? I sniffily asked myself. The answer, of course, was a man who rose at 6.15, cooked himself breakfast, stoked the boiler before spending the day in physical labour on a building site then returning for a meal and an hour or two of paperwork in his office. I was aware of this. But in my arrogance did I truly know it?

My post-homework study course included the arts programme *Monitor* whose profile interviews and films introduced me to Henry Moore, T.H. White, Shelagh Delaney, Sidney Nolan and many more. It was a short television documentary that brought me to the poetry of Robert Frost. The film offered pictures as the poet read,

When I see birches bend to left and right
Across the lines of straighter darker trees,
I like to think some boy's been swinging them..."

and,

Something there is that doesn't love a wall
That sends the frozen-ground-swell under it,
And spills the upper boulders in the sun;
And makes gaps even two can pass abreast..."

He has been a favourite ever since. At Phil and Jim, to give it its due, we had read John Masefield's "Cargoes" and "Sea Fever" as schools did in those days. Also Ralph Hodgson's

See an old unhappy bull
Sick in soul and body both..."

It's a longish poem about the former leader of the herd, dreaming of the glories of yesterday and it often comes to mind when sacked politicians, ex-television executives and "in-my-dayers" in general grumble about what they are no longer in charge of and won't face that their time is over and done with.

I read some of the First World War poets and loved Thomas Hardy, the sadder the better. My own occasional efforts leaned more to John Keats of the odes, the heart aching for the not close enough bosom-friend, convinced that beauty was truth and vice versa.

Testosterone had a hairier chested influence on the novels I read. It was an era of American Second World War epics and I consumed Irwin Shaw's *The Young Lions* and Norman Mailer's *The Naked and the Dead*. I was no tough guy but as with westerns there was a swagger to one's sense of self when reading about them. A war book of a quite different kind, Robert Graves' *Goodbye to All That*, an account of his upbringing and his experiences as an officer in the First World War, made me think hard about the commanding classes, about growing up, about the trust I could place in official histories.

Somewhere in a magazine I read a page or so of desultory dialogue comprising a short play by Harold Pinter and thought, "I could do that." So I wrote a scene between two boys on a bus chatting and arguing in a vaguely sinister manner about girls and work and submitted it to the school magazine. Bob Stanier rejected it as not the kind of thing the magazine printed, but he was good enough to send it to the poet and novelist Cecil Day-Lewis, his friend since they played scrum and fly halves for Wadham College. When Bob heard back he wrote to me: "Dear Wyatt, I enclose your returned article. Mr Day Lewis wrote to me, 'I like this: the chap has a remarkably good ear for a certain desperate kind of talk. It's a bit too short and slight for most mags - I should think the best bet would be *John O'London's*.' I thought you would like to hear this, whether you decide to send it to *John O'London's* or not." He added advice to the innocent, "If you do, it would probably have a slightly better chance if typed - and if typed there should be a spare front sheet with nothing on but the title and your name and address." I did as he suggested and posted it but *John O'London's* were unimpressed and the curtain came down on my career as a playwright even before rehearsals had begun.

I became dimly aware that the more I learned, the more I understood how little I knew of the world. The school had two orchestras and a new music club, the Bach Gesellschaft, a fraternity of the elect, or so I inferred. Of this music I knew nothing. Friends found huge pleasure in playing and listening to classical music. I was missing something and sought entry. I asked the leading musician in my year, Roger Golder, where I should start. He was quite clear, the Brandenburg Concertos, firstly number three. So I bought my first classical LP, the third Brandenburg in an unlikely Deutsche Grammophon coupling with Brahms' alto rhapsody and his variations on a theme by Haydn. Golder advised shrewdly and I quickly purchased the full set of Brandenburgs conducted by Harry Newstone. What next, I asked? Brahms' second symphony was the interesting reply. When Chris Bishop's school recording of the St John Passion in English was offered on disc, I bought one. Most of my records in following years were rock and roll but I had opened the door to a new palace of wonders as a seventeen-year-old should, a palace I would return to.

Where did I think I was going? Probably away from the town and towards the gown. My accent was slowly changing. "Garridge" had not yet moved to "gararge" and it was still a "noospaper" I read but I was brought up short when an English essay was returned with the word "airs" circled in red. I had intended "ours". I took note. It must have been around this time that "garn" became "gone". I only thought about this intermittently. The milieu I was gliding towards was one where people spoke with received pronunciation, as I wouldn't then have called it. It was how my teachers spoke. People referred to "an Oxford accent" in a way that no-one does today. To me that was an exaggeratedly posh voice, loud and drawling, seeking attention. I think I merely wanted to fit in to the world of the educated, to gentrify myself. Street cred carried no premium then. One sought to acquire rather than throw off the badges of status and education. If there was a journey to be travelled, it was upwards.

Mine had begun with Mum's lessons on table manners, on not talking with your mouth full, on not leaving a tide mark round one's neck when washing, keeping shoes clean, shaking hands, looking up to the gentry. Now, I was keeping watch for myself. How do I look? How do I sound? How am I doing?

Yet at the same time I could mock such pretentions. When a school seven a side rugby tournament took place in Oxford, MCS did not enter as it was our hockey term. We went along to watch. Our attention, in particular Pem's attention, was caught by the parents of Solihull School trumpeting the name of the school as they cheered on their boys. "Come orn Sohly Harll." Pem, born a Brummie, was contemptuous: "Everyone in Birmingham calls it 'SollyUll'," he said. We were miffed at not being in a tournament we believed we would have starred in and irritated by the self-satisfied bawling. So, we stood close to the parents and bellowed "Come on SollyUll" in the ugliest Brummie accents we could summon. This, we hoped to imply, was the true spirit of Solihull.

Another spirit I was wrestling with at this time was the holy one. After being confirmed I took communion two or three times with Mum and Dad at Easter. Chief interest was the first taste of red wine, as until then only a sip of unblessed Sauternes had passed my lips. The wafer that accompanied it was like the top half of a flying saucer sweet, minus the sherbet. I was increasingly untouched by any spirituality. God had always presented difficulties. When small, I said my prayers as a little ritual in the knowledge that God was the go-to person to keep everything alright. I accepted that he was everywhere, heard everything and knew everyone's thoughts because the vicar and teachers told me so. On the rare moments I dwelt on this I found it worrying. At church, it was put into specific threatening words, "…to whom all hearts are open, all desires known and from whom no secrets are hidden..." Blimey! I felt generally guilty as I suppose we were meant to. But if all this listening and knowing were true it didn't appear to make much difference to the way people behaved. Any sins I had in mind I just went ahead and committed, possibly feeling a bit bad about it afterwards. That was that. Had Oxford experienced an earthquake, perhaps I would have ascribed the disaster to my being unkind to my brother or looking at the girls' knickers under the table.

When in my late teens I actually listened to the words in chapel or church - all that beseeching, praising, pleading, thanking and hallowing - all I could hear was the vicar making stuff up in elaborate language, apparently confident that what was being asked for would come about. I began to hear only whistling in the wind. It was the words that began to drain me of belief: promised mercy, love and grace but only accessed by endless apologising for being alive. I did wonder if there might be something out there, not the God of the Bible but some other nebulous concept behind everything. That was its difficulty: immortal, invisible and without a hint it existed. I was much impressed by Gilbert Murray's essay, *Pagan Religion and Philosophy*, placing early Christianity in the context of the time it originated. "All the main articles of Christian faith and practice were already latent in the ancient religion... conceptions like The Good Shepherd, the Mother and Child, the worship of a divine Baby, the halo round the head of saints, and innumerable other incidents of the Christian tradition, were of course not new inventions but things ancient and familiar... that a Son of God by a mortal woman, conceived in some spiritual way, and born for the saving of mankind, was at least as old as the fifth century BC." And much more. I felt scales dropping from my eyes. None of this prevented me, then or since, from loving the churches, cathedrals, candlelit evensong and choral music, created to give expression to Christianity.

OXFORD BOY

When John Kennedy emerged as the likely Democratic candidate for the 1960 presidential election I was initially against his selection because he was a Catholic and, as I thought, would be a prisoner of the Pope, owing obedience to the Vatican. On visits to some of the great churches in France I felt the seductive appeal of what I recorded as Catholicism's "beauty, mysticism and surety". The institution, however, I saw as corrupt, greedy and restricting freedom, holding sway over the private and professional lives of its adherents. Did this result from study of the Reformation, in John Stuart Mill's words, "the great and decisive contest against priestly tyranny for liberty of thought"? From learning of Mary Tudor's bonfire of martyrs, the cruelties of the Counter-Reformation, the temporal power of the mediaeval papacy? Possibly, and I certainly thought that anyone who could convince followers of the doctrine of transubstantiation would be capable of putting any dangerous nonsense in people's minds. In fact, by my mid-teens I was suspicious of dogma of any kind, religious or political, anything you signed up to, by which you might concede authority over actions or thoughts. Catholicism along with Communism were the most prominent of such, the one decked in pomp and luxury, the other manifest in tyranny and double think, both controlling and repressive. As yet, I hadn't met enough Catholics, "left footers" as Dad would have called them, to know that many assiduously attended the rituals while taking selective notice of the Church's teachings in their private lives. Especially if you were rich and powerful like the Kennedys.

The first political argument I remember was with my father at the time of the Suez invasion. He complained that never before had we gone to war with an opposition not supporting the government; I countered that this was not disloyalty on behalf of Hugh Gaitskell, the Labour leader, but rashness on the part of Anthony Eden, the prime minister, who should not have invaded Egypt with the nation divided. In the sixth form, I could and did subscribe at a discounted rate to *The Spectator*, generally a Conservative magazine but critical of the government and socially liberal. Its star columnist was Bernard Levin, who wrote about politics with coruscating wit in a way I found both daring and utterly to my taste. I read *The Hidden Persuaders* by Vance Packard, identifying the techniques by which the American advertising industry created wants and manipulated us into satisfying them, everything from the cunning ways supermarkets placed products on shelves to the use of subliminal advertising. I was put on alert as to the practices of big business. I chose Packard's next book, *The Status Seekers*, about America's class system, as my prize for English.

Out of such reading, and probably in response to my parents being lifelong Conservatives, I identified myself on the left. There were the odd moments when I was attracted by the need to break eggs to make the omelette of universal fairness but I was generally a soft socialist. I would never have faced up to it at the time but I think my stance was less driven by idealism than by envy. I was passionate about "equality of opportunity", by which I meant opportunity for me and boys and girls like me. It was certainly unfair that some were poor and some rich, what's more particularly unfair that, though never poor, I was not included in the rich. At some of the public schools we played I bridled at the bigger, more confident boys and their easy loud talk. Did I want to bring such privilege crashing down or did I merely wish that I had it and was that self-confident?

Newspapers liked to write of how we were a generation being brought up in the shadow of the H bomb, "1000 times stronger than the bomb dropped on Hiroshima". This made it sound as if we were bravely undertaking a hazardous adventure when we had no choice and lost no sleep over it. I was creeping towards the Campaign for Nuclear Disarmament, though I had to leave Oxford and a headmaster who was a member before I joined. I was not soft in the head about this, as a letter I wrote to my brother David reassures me: "As for CND, the Communists of course infiltrate any organisation which might be swung to their advantage." The next sentence indicates in a preachy way where I was heading, "This does not necessarily discredit the campaign itself."

My friends and I had earnest conversations about such things but not as many as earnest conversations about sport, television and music. These began to take place in pubs. We favoured The Gardeners Arms in Plantation Road which served the cheapest pint, a shilling as I recall. If we were out for a pub crawl we met at The White Horse in Broad Street and would take in the tucked away Turf Tavern. Many Saturday nights I spent at home in term time. There were occasional dances, "hops" as Mum called them. I loved jiving to Buddy Holly, the Everly Brothers and Chuck Berry. The disc jockey as such was yet to be invented outside of the radio but somebody must have had a record player, speakers and vinyl to play. If there was a live music it would often be a trad jazz band. If someone gave a party, the church halls of Wolvercote or St Michael's, Summertown, were the venues. Out of my sight were parties and formal dances given in large gothic villas for dons' children, black tie and invitation only. I went to few parties in people's houses. A notable one took place at Richard Warnock's while his parents were away. His father was an agreeable man who said nothing when once he caught me peeing in the alley behind their house. He was the best kind of old style bank manager, at Barclays on Banbury Road, near Gee's the florists then, restaurant now. The family lived above the bank which served the good widows, spinsters and academics of

Park Town and the rest of Norham Manor. I doubt that he or his customers ever heard of how Barney Butcher climbed out of the second-floor window above the bank and pissed in full view of the street into the entrance area below to the cheers of those within. This was about as wild as it got. I never saw or heard of anyone smoking cannabis. Purple Hearts were written about in the press and now and then someone would say they knew of people who had some. I never saw any and wouldn't have known what they were for. There was word of a party in a house off Five Mile Drive when a succession of boys visited a young girl in a bedroom and did it. This was never confirmed. The police did not, as rumoured, investigate.

None of my friends had sisters and the first girls I knew were from Milham Ford School, the girls' grammar equivalent of the City of Oxford High School for Boys. The ones I met were well brought up offspring of the lower middle classes. A similar background to mine. To call them homely would make them sound unattractive, which they were not, but homely they were, girls who would help with domestic chores in rubber gloves and pink-nylon house coats. Exactly the kind of girls whom Mum hoped I would mix with. My first girlfriend was Sue Plummer or "Plum", a warm and kindly Milham Ford girl a couple of years younger than me. We met with her friend Wendy and another boy and walked in Cutteslowe Park holding hands but thinking of more. As we strolled under some trees we stopped and I asked, "May I?" She indicated yes and we kissed. I thought that was what you did. You couldn't just presume, could you? I took Plum to the school film show, the safest of dates, when a vintage film (a Will Hay comedy, I am sure) was screened in Big School to an audience on canvas stacking chairs. I noticed as we took our seats that the canvas of my seat had a slight tear, a tear which my weight and my efforts to pull Plum closer widened embarrassing rip by embarrassing rip until it completely gave way and I slipped to the floor. This was a romance on which Cupid scattered no golden arrows and we stepped out for only a few weeks. I do know that my gentlemanly question about the kiss was thought a great joke by Sue and her next, and long-term, boyfriend. Her parents were well off, lived in a house on a double plot on Blandford Avenue, which actually had a swimming pool in the garden. This was a huge attraction as was Plum's battery driven 45rpm portable record player. Transistor radios were becoming popular but this machine was a breakthrough, the Apple IPhone 7 of its day. We could actually play our own records anywhere, even on a hired motor launch on the Thames.

I would like to say there were so many other girls that I cannot name them all but that may not be true. I had an eye for the more exotic. I didn't even know the much talked of Wilma Beechey, but how could you be unaware of a girl with a name like that and a long blond ponytail flying behind her as she cycled to and from Greycotes School? I went out a few times with Jill Brookfield, from the independent Headington School, a quiet, beautiful girl with dark, sad eyes and long black hair in a single plait. There were one or two others.

I was developing a hankering for "posh totty." This may have been influenced by my youthful *tendresse* for the well-spoken Jennifer Gay on children's television. Or family admiration for the gentry entering my loins as well as head. Oxford High School for Girls, a direct grant school like Magdalen, was where goddesses were to be found, dashing brainy daughters of brainy parents. One such I saw speak at a Council for World Citizenship joint schools meeting, Miriam Margolyes, who lived not far from me, an unmissable girl with a flare of long black curly hair exploding from under her hat. I knew of her as she was friendly with Mrs H, Uncle Walter's what we would now call partner, then common law wife. Both were extrovert and interestingly eccentric.

There was a desirable group of younger goddesses whom I took to be dons' daughters and most likely out of my league. Among them were Julia Lumsden, short, with a sensual rather than beautiful face whom I believed to be at the epicentre of Oxford party life; long legged, glamorous Pamela Church, and clever, shapely, Monica Mendelssohn, whom I did go out with a few times. Along with another couple, she and I memorably shared a punt overnight, freezing though wrapped in blankets, to be in position with our breakfast picnic for the May morning hymn from Magdalen Tower. There was another quite lovely girl, a philosopher's daughter, three years younger than me but so much more sophisticated. She enjoyed coming out with John Martin and me. My saintly dad allowed me to drive his new Austin pickup at weekends so we could travel out of Oxford to rumoured or real parties and she would join us. Sometimes we would pick her up from her house which, as it happened, faced on to the cobble stones of Merton Street. She had a boyfriend she'd met at a black tie North Oxford party but he was away at school somewhere. I should have taken heed when she described him as looking like Jacques Charrier, the French film star, about as unlike me as a man could look, but I made the error of declaring myself in a letter. Her reply dropped my heart to the floor. She was not interested. As she put it, "I thought you were quite happy just to be a beefy pal…" No, boys usually aren't. And I wasn't even all that beefy. So this was what all those poems and songs were about.

It was back to getting off with girls at parties, which had its definite pleasures. Being enveloped in the thick smell of powder and scent that exploded in the jive and hung stickily close in the slow dances. Holding damp palm to damp palm. Learning by trial and error the design principles and engineering of the brassiere. Confused fumbling among frothy petticoats, exploring the well defended territory beneath. Achieving the occasional advance to silky pastures above the stocking tops. A happy tangle with a blonde Dutch girl in a park in Arnhem on a day visit from RAF camp.

I sought to improve my appeal by close attention to dress. Summer rig for school allowed an open neck white shirt, enabling a sartorial statement to be made. Instead of having the shirt collar flap limply on the blazer lapel, you could turn up the points so they stood proud by the ear. I rejected this as striving too hard and opted instead for a preppy effect, the collar folded down neatly inside the jacket. I was not so cool that I did not enjoy strutting my stuff in the black piping, school crest and elaborate gothic lettering of the rugby colours blazer. I liked grey trousers and even for just tootling out to town for coffee usually wore a jacket and tie. I made the stylish purchase of a suede jacket and affected a polo shirt buttoned to the neck under a V neck sweater or jacket. I needed a suit not least to wear for entrance exams. I chose one in a dark blue and slightly paler blue stripe. The jacket buttoned high - four buttons - with short, narrow lapels and the trousers drainpipe. The latter I asked Mum to take in even further and wore them with black Chelsea boots with Cuban heels. A shirt with small rounded collar and a narrow tie completed this vision of hopefulness.

Mum was herself a great clothes shopper. For several years, she took the train to London a month before Christmas to meet her cousin Edie for a shopping expedition. The rendezvous was always the main entrance to Selfridges, about as grand as things got, we thought. In time Dad drove us all up to see the Oxford Street lights and have lunch at a Lyons Corner House. Mum was more confident these days and liked to catch the bus into Oxford to have coffee in the Cadena or Elliston's with one or two other Magdalen mothers. We were noticeably better off now and when it came to celebrate Mum and Dad's 25th wedding anniversary, they arranged dinner for twenty or more relations and friends at the Weston Manor Hotel. I was to propose the toast and searched copies of *Reader's Digest* for what passed as jokes. I raised the odd laugh but more importantly said the sort of things I should about my parents. Given the number of Hoopers present there was quite a bit of silent tucking in to the food as conversation over a meal did not come naturally. Then suddenly the chomping was interrupted and even the taciturn Hoopers cried out as Aunty Phyl, grimacing and hissing noisily, tensed and fell off her chair to the floor. Her daughter Anne had been a nurse, was not fussed and knew what to do. Uncle Ron was calm as well. They had seen this before. Phyl was soon restored and we learned that she was an epileptic but had not had a seizure for twenty years.

Much as I loved family occasions I had the previous year observed one of youth's rites of passage when I passed on the family holiday to go away with friends. I think David was probably more disappointed than my parents as they returned to a family hotel in Newquay from which an excited David sent me a card, "I won 35/- at Bingo on Friday. It's the party tonight..." I joined the Youth Hostel Association, "profession - schoolboy", for a cycling trip to Holland with Richard Warnock, Duncan Kilgour and Adam "Barney" Butcher, the last of these a serious cyclist. Richard and I set off together, a significant enough departure in life for it to be photographed. As international travellers, we were still probationers as a card home indicated: "had a bit of a job finding our way out of Littlemore, and Nock's chain came off just before Nuneham

Courtenay at about twenty past nine." Undaunted, "we didn't stop again till Old Windsor, where we both had a pint of bitter." We stopped overnight at Kemsing youth hostel and the other two arrived to meet us at Dover the following day. The card home from Dover boasted, "the money is going pretty well and I am well within my limit." He spoke too soon.

We chose Holland for cycling as it was flat. So it was, but because of that it was also, as we discovered, windy, especially as we pedalled head down alongside the dikes. We were diligent tourists, seeing The Hague, Scheveningen, Rotterdam, Harlem, Nijmegen and Amsterdam. I have the dim memory of us walking by red lit windows gawking shyly at large women in lacy slips who, even to randy seventeen year olds, were as appetising as a greengrocer's window full of bruised Bramleys. We returned on the ferry to Harwich and, on landing, split up. Nock, the bank manager's son, had husbanded his funds carefully and bought a rail ticket to Oxford for him and his bike. The rest of us had just a shilling or two each. There was nothing for it but to ride 150 miles overnight in the chilly September air through the silent deserted centres of St Alban's and Hertford. Nearing Oxford we spotted a milkman on his round and could afford a bottle each.

The following year Richard Warnock and I went hitchhiking in France. It was perfectly possible in those times to plan journeys confident drivers would pick you up. We stayed mainly in youth hostels. In one, we slept in a huge dormitory of bunk beds, when as the lights had just been turned out a rich American voice announced, "Anyone who can guess what's in my hand can have a bite." I heard no rush of feet in his direction. Possibly they tiptoed. In Paris, we stayed in a cheap hotel near the Opéra and saw the things we should on a first visit. We went via Rouen to the coast at Le Touquet, winning one long lift in a comfortable car with a Frenchman and his seventeen-year-old daughter. She gave me her address and on return we conducted a correspondence touching on books, films and politics. Her brother was doing his national service in Algeria, where a fierce war for independence had been raging. President de Gaulle believed that Algeria should be governed by the Algerians, angering the French settlers who fought the French gendarmerie. My views were standard anti-colonial and were politely contested in the letters I received, then more firmly contested, then no more letters. I couldn't work out if it was due to the photograph I had sent, at her request (Oh, crikey, had she thought she was writing to Richard?). Or had I gone too far in my views on the Algerian War? The self-doubt of youth nagged away.

I couldn't afford to be distracted. In those days, it was usual to stay for a third year in the sixth form as university places were mostly contested in the term after A Levels. Entrance was decided by interviews and exams conducted just before or after Christmas. I was measuring myself for a gown somewhere. Did I wish to remain an Oxford boy in gown as well as town?

The Gentlemen of Song.
Left to right, Back: Roger
Golder, Desmond Cecil,
WW, John Cooke. Front:
Julian Starmer-Smith,
Tim Hunt, Robert "Sherb"
Herbertson.

14

FROM THE DARK TO THE LIGHT

Naturally, Mum had designated A Level exams as precious metal, each golden ball now larger than its predecessor. She had her own ideas of how to help me perform well, insisting I drank a glass of Guinness or port of an evening "to build up your strength". I knuckled down. In August friends who did holiday work in the exam schools told me I had distinctions in English and History well before the postcard arrived with the official results. I failed Latin, no surprise there and no problem as long as I had sufficient residue of the language to tackle an unseen. The distinctions augured well for what was to come and secured me a state scholarship.

My schooling was linked to a college, had been nourished by the institutions around it and was imbued with the values of the university. For all that, the university was not my Oxford, I knew that you could never take Oxford out of the boy but you could take the boy out of Oxford. I liked the idea of going to Cambridge. I was the least adventurous of souls but would be nineteen by the time I went up and it felt a bit lame to remain in the same city. Sooner or later I knew I would move away. This seemed the moment. The school's priority was for me to win an award if I was able. Open entry exhibitions (good) and scholarships (better) were highly prized in those days (long since dropped). They were awarded by the colleges, were few in number and came with money and, most importantly for the school, trailing a cloud of glory. Hence the emphasis; hence the honours boards in Big School. The school understandably had good contacts at several Oxford colleges and it was put to me that if I secured a place but no award at Cambridge I should then sit for a scholarship at Oxford. I was not minded to do this but kept that to myself.

When "Sid" Millward had left to take up a headmastership, he was replaced by Dr Peter Brooks, the first Cambridge historian on the staff. He was engaging, clever, slightly camp and laughed a lot, behaving as if we were all in a great conspiracy with him, a conspiracy as he saw it against the rest of the staff. He had an eccentric side. Junior boys reported that he employed the "thunderclap" as part of his teaching armoury, this requiring a boy in short trousers to stand on a desk while Brooks rapped a wooden ruler back and forth between his knees. The boys thought it a huge joke. Dr Brooks was an ecclesiastical historian and a friend of another such, David Newsome, the director of studies in history at Emmanuel College. When I said I was interested in Cambridge, Brooks suggested I apply there. The good doctor has since written books on the Reformation and Cranmer in particular, as well as a biography of his Siamese cat, Nimrod. We did not rate him highly as a teacher but we did value his imitations of old parsons, tales of "Jolly Jack" Plumb at Cambridge and essays he set on French nuclear tests, capital punishment, Marx and the like. "Aunty Brooks" was a stimulating presence, quite different in style and interests from other history masters we had known.

I had by now received a letter from The Master, "Dear Wyatt…", appointing me a school prefect, a role I was keen to take as it elevated me to the aristocracy of our little nation state. The letter laid on the gravitas a little thickly: "…loyalty to your colleagues and to all members of staff and to the best interests of the school and also constant vigilance and devotion to duty…." I am sure I took this very seriously at the time. I was a believer. One of the school's most fervent believers was Dennis Clarke, classics master. Bustling, always in a hurry carrying a sheaf of papers, he spoke fast and on the run, his curl of grey hair bobbing. Denis had been a boy at MCS and radiated kindliness and love of the institution. He ran the old boys' club and updated Bob Stanier's history of the school. Like the best of teachers, he was an all-rounder, singing tenor in the choir, a setter of crossword puzzles and a winner in the *Spectator's* competitions. In the final terms I was one of a group who would cycle up to his house for discussions and play readings, among them Auden and Isherwood's *The Ascent of F6*. Somehow one knew that Dennis was a carrier of the everlasting flame.

I was assigned as prefect, and Tim Hunt as house prefect, to Maltby 3 houseroom. The house tutor was a new master, Peter Needham, "an amusing but slack type unless I am mistaken" was my snooty first impression. He was a classicist who would screw up his face and affect a grumpy schoolmaster demeanour, whereas he was in fact a fount of good humour and friendliness. "Boy" or a loud "Boyee" was his regular mode of address. He would give an elaborate performance of exasperated ill temper, making jokey asides in a stage whisper. He offered advice should I be caught by National Service, "Slip a corporal two and six to get off bog bashing". Perhaps because he did not actually teach me, I related to him less as a teacher, more as a friend, which he became. Peter had come to Britain with the Kindertransport from Czechoslovakia. He taught for the remainder of his career at Eton and translated two Harry Potter books into Latin, "an ideal job for an old bloke in retirement". Two small boys in that houseroom were Munby, now Sir James, President of the Family Division of the High Court, and Ellis, Sir Vernon, Chair of the British Council.

I had a new base in the prefects' study, a smallish room at the end of one of the old single-storey concrete blocks. We each had a locker and there were a few tables and chairs. In the corner a pile of lost property clothing silently composted. Prefects were responsible for day-to-day rule-keeping and for punishing offenders. We had three sanctions: telling off, lines and beating. I used the first extensively and the second I thought moderately, although a list of names in the back of a term diary reveals not that moderately (the still unknighted Ellis being one of several owing 100 lines). The third was not for me. Before a beating took place the prefect was required to enter the name of the transgressor in the beating log along with his offence and the number of strokes. Three was usual, the maximum I think five. A second prefect was needed to sign as a witness. My name only appeared in that log as an offender in my first years, for I never beat a boy and refused to witness another prefect doing so. I was not against corporal punishment per se but I thought it wrong for boys to be beating other boys, especially when the victim might be fifteen or even sixteen and the beater only a year or so older. I was in a minority of one among the prefects, one or two of whom I thought enjoyed this task a little more than they should have.

We had fun in that small study, too. One boy taught us bridge which was in vogue for a while. We had a dart board and someone brought in a reel to reel tape recorder. On this we recorded our version of *Grandstand*, the Saturday afternoon television sports programme. I played Yorkshireman Eddie Waring the Rugby League commentator, "It's Wigann versus Sayn Tellens…. the lad's gone for an early bath." And added Blackpool boxer Brian London after his memorable interview with Harry Carpenter, "Well, 'Arry, I hit 'im with every 'ook in the book." Someone clicked his mouth to provide snooker ball accompaniment to another's impersonation of commentator "Whispering" Ted Lowe. We started a syndicate to enter the football pools each week and planned what we would do with the winnings - "Come to school in sedan chairs with motor cycle outriders."

Apart from a crescendo of revision and extra work ahead of Oxbridge exams, this was a busy term of organising coaches, oranges and touch judges, and more importantly playing, for the all-conquering rugby side. The Shakespeare performance was *Henry VI Part 2*, an odd one to choose but I presume it was on the English syllabus. The ineffectual Henry was Viv Brooke, a tall, very blond and gentle boy who became a doctor. The livewire Tom Wheare, later headmaster of Bryanston, was the wicked Suffolk. Most memorable was Pem as a Brummie-accented Jack Cade, leader of the rebels, one of whom I played as well giving a comic turn as Thomas Horner the Armourer, praised by the *Oxford Mail* reviewer in a cutting I kept. Dear old Wettoe the co-director was plastered throughout the evening. One or two chums and I became The Gentlemen of Song, dressed in boaters, bow ties and waistcoats, to sing music hall songs. Roger Golder was the musician at the piano, Des Cecil as Gypsy Desmondo played the violin and five of us sang, of whom two, Tim Hunt and John Cooke, could actually sing while Robert Herbertson, Julian Starmer-Smith and I did our best. I devised some moves and hand gestures and off we went with

Hello, hello, hello Susie Green,
Come along quickly do,

and,

Hello, hello, who's your lady fiend,
Who's the little girlie by your side?...
It isn't the girl I saw you with at Brighton.
Who, who, who's your lady friend?

Half way through our performances I performed a series of funny walks to the tune of "Colonel Bogey". We stormed the parents' association's annual knees up, several Women's Institutes and with breath-taking chutzpah provided the cabaret at the rowdy Oxford Rugby Club dinner.

I was girding my loins for the Emmanuel scholarship examination when I received a letter from Mr Gray, the headmaster from Phil and Jim, who had moved away from Oxford and with whom my parents had evidently kept in touch. He congratulated me on my A Levels: "news like this always makes a schoolmaster happy particularly in this instance when I feel that 'Phil & Jim' laid the foundation stone of your achievement..." Now, "foundation stone" may have been a fair compliment to the teaching at Phil and Jim but would not do for the ruse most likely instrumental in lifting me to Magdalen. Reading this back I think the word "ruse" is a true but hardly emphatic enough description of Mr Gray's, and my, malpractice. "Skulduggery"? - too heroic a tinge. "Hanky-panky"? - means something else these days. "Fiddle"? - sounds like one of the Wyatt family's horse racing scams. I think it has to be "cheating" and have done with it. Did the dark deed step guiltily forward to nag me when I received the letter? I don't think so. I had long marked it "not wanted on voyage" and stowed it below.

My attention was on what Mr Gray wrote next. I bridled as he sought to redirect me, "You are an Oxford boy, you have done well at the foremost boys' school in Oxford. Perhaps if you went up to an Oxford College and did equally well you could take up university teaching and then there would be literally no limit to your climb to fame. Think of all the leaders of today who were originally Oxford dons." Apart from his making far too many assumptions, this was his plan, not mine. "How dare he?" I thought. Reading the letter now with its apologetic conclusion, "Just a thought - after all you have done more than I ever could," I can see no harm. In truth, he had lit the blue touch paper, albeit with a stolen box of matches.

I took the train to Cambridge for the scholarship exams in my sharp suit and Cuban heels feeling "bloody nervous". You changed at Bletchley where I sat on the cold December afternoon with my history notes. I alighted at Cambridge on the platform where two years later I was to first clap eyes on my wife. A bus took me to Emmanuel where I reported to the Senior Tutor's office. Here sat several other candidates whose measure I tried to gauge. Two of them were talking together in voices which marked them to my open, generous mind as "public school shits". One had something of the fleshy Oscar Wilde about him, the other was his antithesis, tall and thin with the air of one who had not only already secured entrance but was about take up a fellowship. I sent whatever malevolent vibes I could muster.

I had an interview with the Senior Tutor, Peter Hunter Blair, whom I remember as a handsome man of great age (he was 48). He explained the timetable and I was directed under the tunnel to my allocated room in North Court. A skeleton stood welcomingly in the corner as the room was normally inhabited by a medical student. He had left a note to the candidate it might concern, wishing good luck. On the mantelpiece above the gas fire was the Cambridge Union programme for the term just ended with a proud "Me" written alongside his name as seconder of a motion. I was impressed. With the fire on it was a cosy room, and I tried to imagine student life here. A few other MCS boys were applying to different colleges and I had made a date with them to meet for a drink at The Mitre near St John's. This was a helpful plan, taking the mind off the tournament to come. What's more, making my way through the dark and chilly streets to meet friends in a new pub was almost like being a real undergrad.

The tournament was over three days comprising a three hour essay, a general paper, two history papers and a Latin unseen followed by an interview with David Newsome. I felt I performed pretty well with a good essay on the very Oxbridge question, "What was not restored at the Restoration?" Newsome, who had taught at Wellington College and was later to be Master there, was probing but friendly. He had a shiny round face and a companionable air. The book lined room, lit by table and standard lamps, was quiet save for the buzzing of the gas fire. This was exactly how I imagined a Cambridge don's room. I hoped for the best and left feeling fairly confident only to miss the train, which went from the wrong platform, and had to travel via London arriving home at one o'clock.

A few days later, on the penultimate day of term, the phone rang in the evening with a telegram message. "Congratulations Minor Scholarship Emmanuel = Senior Tutor." This was well before the days of punching the air, shouting "RESULT" and jumping about high fiving, but something like that was going on inside. I had not expected as much. I gave Mum and Dad the good news. I hope I gave her a hug and a kiss. Next I rang Mr Arnold-Craft at home.

"Sir, it's Wyatt."

"Yes, Alan?" (he always called me Alan).

"I've got a minor scholarship at Emmanuel."

"A scholarship, Alan. Are you sure?"

I think he had caught a note of triumphalism in my voice. I read the telegram to him. A confirming letter from Emmanuel followed. I had been awarded the Gerald Campbell Owen scholarship which I was tickled to discover from his memoir, was held a few years after by David Ashforth, one of Britain's best and funniest racing writers. The school's honours board would get its name; I would be spared pressure to sit further exams. Cambridge it was to be.

Mum remembered how all this had begun and unknown to me sent a telegram to Mr Gray. I bet it did not say, "Thanks for fiddling the eleven plus." She had spread the word further, for a card arrived from Christ Church, Oxford, with congratulations from Dr and Mrs Heaton with whom she had been in service in Oxford and at Garsington Manor. My joy increased with the news that Tim Hunt was accepted at Clare, Cambridge, and John Cooke had won an exhibition to King's, laying foundations for what were to be lifelong friendships. The bow string drawn back seven years earlier had landed its arrow almost on the bullseye. Its flight was hardly unconventional but it was my arrow and unique. To my parents it was probably better than they could have hoped for when I was born. Then, a collar and tie job for their son, indoors in a bank or office, would have been enough to show that the Wyatts were on the move. Did a second letter from Mr Gray now nag my memory of how I had passed the eleven plus well enough to get me to Magdalen? Serene as I was in my own success, I don't think it did. It was not mentioned by my parents while I was at school nor ever afterwards.

Two remaining school terms awaited, opportunity for laps of honour and a gentle work regime. I went back for one. Dr Brooks proclaimed to the history set, a propos my destination, that Cambridge was the finest way to finish a person's education, to which Pem, not an admirer of Brooks, commented, "Well, it certainly finished his." I had passed my driving test and Dad let me have the car now and then so I could show off by driving our Morris Oxford to school, parking in Cowley Place. Some of us took to sloping off to The Temple pub at lunchtimes for a pint and a game of darts, unbeknown, as we imagined, to the teachers. I researched, wrote and delivered a paper for the historical society on Wyatt's Rebellion, a serious task that also achieved the hoped for hilarity when announced at assembly. I was treading water before I left at Easter.

Bob Stanier gave a leavers' talk, wishing us good fortune in whatever careers we chose as long as it was not advertising. Perhaps he had also read *The Hidden Persuaders*. More likely, he had the Oxbridge academic distaste for manipulating people - as he might have seen it - for financial advantage. This influenced me as well. It was something of a tribute to Bob, his example and his values that at least half a dozen of my vintage became teachers, two becoming deputy heads at Reeds, Cobham and Wellington, and three from the following year heads at Bradfield, Bryanston and Christ's Hospital. My default setting was that the only proper jobs for graduates were in universities, schools, writing and journalism. This was not uncommon and was at the heart of what was so much wrong with Britain for a long time. In spite of Dad's business I was ignorant of the wider commercial world and, through snobbery and lack of curiosity, content to be so.

I began transitioning from Oxford. An indication that my allegiance would shortly change came when I played for the Oxford Rugby Club in the Esher seven-a-side tournament, a significant one at the time. One of the star teams, reaching the final, was Emmanuel College Cambridge in their navy blue shirts with thin pink hoops. They looked formidable. What struck me most was the appealing chant of support from their followers, "Come on Emma!" I liked that.

My ambitious plan for the summer was to go to Canada to work, staying with Dad's sister Berta and her husband in Windsor,

Ontario. However, their letters were not encouraging: "It's impossible to line up a job for you. 40% population is either out of work or on short time... Another thing the Labor Unions practically run the plants." They suggested two longshots, "You could try the Forestry Service for the summer - looking for forest fires up North, or as camp counsellor in summer camps. Have you written to Canada house in London?" I had but to no avail.

One way or another, the world of work beckoned and I planned to earn some money then have a holiday. For a month or so I drove a van for Stephenson's builders' merchants, delivering pots of paint and sheets of glass. I liked the independence of the job, especially the sacred mid-morning and lunch breaks when I could park, open *The Daily Telegraph* and enjoy a flask of instant coffee with biscuits or homemade sandwiches.

Believing myself to be more a man of the world than I turned out to be, I found a job as a junior barman in the Barra Hotel, Jersey. Letters back and forth to home tell a tale of an innocent at large. I persuaded Mum that I could afford to eat enough but I was not sleeping well in my grotty digs ("neither place has water in the room and one hasn't got a bathroom"). A mother knew why, because I was "hungry and tired... It is too long to go without food from 6 pm-1 am and then only two sandwiches." I sought to wangle more and better food by ingratiating myself with the chef but without success as he received a cut of everything he saved. I took against Mr Parry, the hotel manager, "He's fat, smokes a cigar and struts about." I didn't have the correct rig and had to write home for my black clip-on bow tie. Parry told me to wear dark trousers, that meant my best pair. Again, Mum was not happy, "I would not wear my best trousers for no-one." I liked being behind the bar but was deficient in bar skills. "You might like to know," I wrote home, where I was famously clumsy, "that I have only broken 4 glasses drying them up and knocked over one drink - not bad at all." The proprietress came in one evening and announced that the hotel needed a proper cocktail barman, so a new man was brought in, the head barman took my place and I became a dogsbody, sweeping up, scrubbing, clearing out bottles and vacuuming in the morning, covering for the day porter in the afternoons. "The main trouble with this," I wrote, "is that it's a deadly bore and I don't get a chance of meeting the girls who are staying here as I did as barman." I was earning £6. 17. 2d per week. I couldn't save more than 10 shillings, whereas at Stephenson's I saved £5 per week. "At this rate," I wrote, "I shall have hardly anything from the £100 I am allowed to earn without Dad being taxed for me."

In truth, I was something of a seven-pound claimer in the world at large. I was also homesick. David missed me and wrote newsy letters, one with an unflattering sketch of what he thought Parry looked like. Dad had won new contracts but wrote to tell me he was worried because he could not hire the men he needed, that lorries had arrived late, an architect failed to turn up for a handover. He added, "I have asked David to get the cricket bat out as I want to give him a few overs of an evening. I will finish now as *The Black and White Minstrels* has just started."

I left the hotel and worked for a week or so in a warehouse packing Jersey potatoes into wooden tubs. I could do better by returning to Oxford. Mum, an expert on the customs allowances, sent me her shopping list: "cigarettes 200 if (Players or Senior Service) ½ bt. Whisky; 1 bottle Champagne; I think you could probably bring another ½ whisky if you opened it and had a little out," then a list of perfumes "(French must be)" and soaps for Christmas presents. It was never too early. I took a couple of days for the beach hoping for a bit of a tan, bought a cheeky little black and white trilby to provide a raffish look and flew home.

Friends were working for Walls Ice Cream delivering to shops and I got a job there as a driver's mate. Also with a summer job at Walls was Ron Atkinson, captain of Oxford United ("The Tank") and later manager of, among others, Manchester United and Atlético Madrid. Driver's mate at Walls was a cushy but not entirely unnecessary job. I liked driving round the villages of North and West Oxfordshire, enjoying the countryside, chatting with the driver, unloading at the stops. The work bit was turning up but I was usually off early for an evening with friends, playing tennis, some evening cricket, swimming and pubbing. I gave several pounds to Mum "for my keep" and was able to save.

We were all tasting the inevitable but little understood life of the workplace. Several worked for the Oxford O and A Level examination boards, a bureaucratic and none too testing environment. Tim Hunt sought a career in science and learned in a university laboratory that such a life had its casualties. "This dept. has a wonderful record: 1 suicide (a D.Phil student), 1 chap carted off to the Warneford during office hours, 1 secretary underwent complete and utter physical and mental breakdown, 2 chief technicians who have both seen the inside of a mental home." We were all discovering that the politics of work differed from those of school. It wasn't necessarily the boss who held the strings of your existence. At Stephenson's, it was the person who determined your route; at Walls, the man who allocated staff to vans; at the lab, the woman who controlled the stationary rations. We suffered the petty tyrants and power battles of the workplace. At the hotel, it was the kitchen versus the bar versus the management; at the lab between the mutually dependent and mutually suspicious academics and technicians. Tim overheard an angry technician, "Just let him say it is not quite right and I'll throw the bloody lot in his face…" as the professor in question crept silently to his room having been listening. Other friends, who didn't but perhaps should have gone into the city, set their brains to wangling lower insurance on the vehicle they were buying. Instead of both being students perhaps one could be the other's professional oboe player, the other the musician's chauffeur. Too clever by half, it transpired.

John Cooke, studying in Heidelberg, was an assiduous sender of postcards. Such were the conventions of the time that the first few I received were signed simply, "Cooke". Slowly, formality was relaxed and they came from "JAC", finally from "John". In Germany, he reported, they had "a system of 'Akademische Freiheit' – i.e. freedom to do no work if you don't want to. I am making full use of this…" He further confessed, "the weather continues very fine and I am going about without a jacket, which as you know is rare for me. yours till the Great Barrel in Hofburg Castle runs dry (221716 litres)."

Towards the end of the summer Dad let me take his work van on a jaunt to the South of France with Pem, Richard Warnock and Julian "Eric" Starmer-Smith. We put up in the hotel in Paris where Richard and I had stayed the previous year and met an American couple from central casting. The wife questioned us seriously and at every answer turned to her husband and asked, "Say Ezra, did you hear that?" Ezra was full of old saws: "No matter how cheap it is if it's not good it's not a bargain.'" The four of us failed to take this advice on board and went to a modestly priced strip show at which all save Eric were soon bored by the repetition. We drove on to Lyon, Gap and the Cote d'Azur, where, as we inched forward in the traffic on the Promenade des Anglais, I looked to a large black saloon alongside and saw the deathly pale head of the aged Winston Churchill gazing blankly out. We slept by the road in a gorge near Toulon where I noted, "awoke still whole, untouched by terrorists, tramps or animals", and a horrid camp site by a stinking lake, threated by malicious-looking Alsatians. On to Arles, Les Baux and Avignon, where we knew that goddesses were nigh. My diary reported, "Called here on the Oxford High School party but they were all in bed at 8.45!! We slept by the side of the N7, once again, within 50 yards of the busy railway."

We returned to prepare for the parting of the ways. Pem was off to Durham University then to teach; Richard to New College, Oxford and a teaching career; John Martin to St Edmund Hall, Oxford and teaching; Robert Herbertson to Corpus Christi, Oxford, then to steel companies in Sheffield and South Africa; Julian Starmer-Smith to Sandhurst, later Colonel 29th Commando; Tex Collier to RAF Cranwell then business; John Cooke and Tim Hunt were joining me at Cambridge, John then to the Civil Service, Tim to a fellowship and a Nobel Prize.

My finances were in good shape. A letter from Bob Stanier offered a small bonus. "Dear Wyatt, you have been awarded an Ogle Scholarship Prize, value £15," adding, "The value has been reduced since last year as winners of Open Awards now receive financial benefit from their college." True, I had £60 per year from Emmanuel. The state scholarship - tax payers - paid my fees as well as a maintenance grant of £322 p.a. (about £6,700 today). Dad was expected to contribute £16. He was more generous.

I shopped in Oxford for my Cambridge uniform. I bought a dark green corduroy jacket from Zacharias, on the corner of Ship Street. I think it was six guineas. Hall Brothers, the dandyish men's shop in The High, provided two grey, green and black striped Madras cotton shirts and a knitted tie. In Queen Street I found dark grey flannel trousers with a raised seam and black jeans with green stitching. The whole ensemble to be wrapped in a navy duffle coat when the colder weather arrived.

Uncle Ron and Auntie Phyl had taken Dad, Mum and me in their Jaguar on a Cambridge recce a few weeks earlier, Phyl shouting excitedly along the way "We're going to see our Alan's digs. Now in early October, Mum, Dad, and David drove me over with my clothes, books and a homemade chocolate sponge in a cake tin. As a scholar, I was allocated a room in brand new student accommodation, Barnwell Hostel, on the Newmarket Road. The smart, modern room was on the ground floor looking onto Midsummer Common and across to the river. The family helped me unload and said goodbye.

I put supplies in a food cupboard, clothes in the drawers and stacked my books – the shelves had yet to be put up. I could hear others moving into their rooms. I would say hello later. In the next-door scholar's room was the man who would provide the link to my wife. Hall dinner was at 6.45 and soon I set off to walk there, college tie clashing with Madras cotton shirt, navy blue and pink college scarf round my neck. As I strode down Maids Causeway, through New Square and across Christ's Pieces, I was making plans. An ex-Cambridge master who had observed my funny walks routine said I should audition for the Footlights. I would. I liked the idea of working on *Varsity*, the student newspaper, so would join that. I decided to put my name down for a college rugby trial. Emma was good at the game and I looked forward to watching teammates play for the university. My loyalties had switched: I was a light blue not a dark blue supporter now. No longer an Oxford boy but, in the language of the time, a Cambridge man.